BOUNDARIES
IN BUSINESS

The Playbook for Mindful Leadership

DeBLAIR TATE

CONTENTS

"BOUNDARIES DON'T PUSH PEOPLE AWAY; THEY PULL YOUR POWER BACK."

MESSAGE FROM THE AUTHOR

Let me start with this — I didn't write this book because I've mastered boundaries or leadership. I wrote it because both of them punched me in the chest more than once.

I've worn a lot of titles in my life — military, coach, business, and yes, co-founder and executive board member of a motorcycle club. I've held every seat on that board. President. Vice. Secretary. Treasurer. Sgt-at-Arms. You name it, I've sat in it.

And if I'm honest, that's where a lot of my lessons about boundaries got real.

People see the patches, the structure, the loyalty — but what they don't see are the long nights, the conflict, the decisions that don't make everybody happy, the weight of being "the one they call." They don't see the moments when you're leading grown adults who all have opinions, egos, lives, and pain — and you're expected to carry it and hold the culture together at the same time.

There were times in that space where I was pouring into everybody else while quietly running on empty. Times where I kept the peace instead of telling the truth. Times where I thought being available 24/7 was leadership, when really I was just disappearing piece by piece. I crossed my own boundaries and then felt frustrated when other people followed my example. That one stung.

The military sharpened my discipline. Coaching sharpened my ability to develop people. The club sharpened my honesty. It forced me to see where I avoided hard conversations, where I tried to fix everything myself, where I held everything together on the outside while I was worn down on the inside.

That's where this book really came from.

Not from "perfect leadership principles." From the nights I sat with myself and had to admit: I can't keep leading like this and calling it strength.

I had to learn that: saying "no" doesn't make you cold having a backbone doesn't make you mean protecting your time isn't selfish and burning yourself out is not loyalty

I have grown, and I'm still growing. I still catch myself slipping into old habits — overdoing, overcommitting, over-carrying. Growth didn't turn me into a different person overnight. It just stopped letting me lie to myself about what it was costing me.

This book is for corporate leaders in boardrooms and leaders who don't have a title at all. For founders. For parents. For coaches. For club presidents and team leads and people everybody leans on "because you're strong."

You may feel uncomfortable reading parts of this. You might feel seen. You might feel called out a little. That's okay. Sit with it. Don't run from it.

All I ask is that while you read, you tell yourself the truth.

Where are you crossing your own boundaries? Where are you shrinking? Where are you carrying everything because you don't trust anyone else to? Where have you stopped growing because being needed feels safer than being honest?

I'm not writing at you. I'm writing with you.

Leadership will expose every crack you try to hide. Boundaries aren't walls — they're the lines that keep you from losing yourself while you're busy taking care of everybody else.

I had to face me first. This book is me saying: I had to face myself… and I think it's time you do too.

Let's talk about what leadership really looks like — without the performance.

"LEADERSHIP ISN'T ABOUT BEING LIKED. IT'S ABOUT BEING CLEAR, CALM, AND ACCOUNTABLE."

INTRODUCTION
REAL LEADERSHIP, REAL TALK

Getting straight to the point—titles don't make leaders. Suits don't make leaders. Big offices with nameplates don't make leaders. Leadership is who you are when the lights are off, when nobody's clapping, and when no one's watching to see if you'll do the right thing. It's how you treat people, how you carry yourself, and how you handle pressure. And if all you're doing is trying to look the part without *being* the part, people will spot it a mile away.

See, leadership isn't about perfection. People don't want a "Perfect Patty" acting like they've never messed up a day in their life. They want somebody real. Somebody human. Somebody who can admit, "Yeah, I don't have it all together, but I'm still showing up." Please know that people don't connect with your mask, they connect with your authenticity.

And connection is the real currency of leadership. People are not machines; they got kids to raise, bills to pay, struggles you can't see on the surface. If you can't slow down and really hear them—like, *actually hear them*—you're not leading, you're just managing. And managers check boxes, but leaders build people. Leaders listen, lean in, and make space. Sometimes the most powerful thing you can do as a leader isn't to speak, but to shut up and really listen.

But don't get it twisted—listening and leading with heart doesn't mean letting people run all over you. Boundaries are part of the job description. If you don't have them, you'll burn out, get bitter, and start resenting the very people you were called to lead. Let me remind you that "No" is a complete sentence. Boundaries don't push people out; they show people how to come in. If you don't set the standard, you'll stay stuck carrying everybody's load while your own life crumbles in the background.

Most people don't want to admit that conflict is inevitable. I don't care how perfect your team looks on paper, there will come a time when people clash. Somebody's feelings will get hurt, somebody's ego will flare up, somebody will test your patience. So, do you run from it, or do you rise up and face it? True leaders don't flinch; they know how to step into conflict and flip it into connection. Conflict, handled with confidence and empathy, can be the glue that pulls your entire team tighter.

Don't let your ego fool you. Leadership is not about being the loudest one in the room, proving a point, or always having the last word. That's small energy. Leaders know how to protect the culture they're building, even when it means having the hard conversations nobody else wants to have. Silence doesn't solve conflict, but it can definitely delay the explosion. You either address it now, or you'll be cleaning up a bigger mess later.

Don't get me wrong—leading can get really messy. People will try you. I mean play right in your face. They'll test your patience, push every button you have known to man, and make you wonder if you're even built for this. You do know that people are mirrors, right? That coworker who stays late talking too loud? Maybe they're reflecting the voice you keep silencing in yourself. That teammate whose desk looks like chaos on wheels? Maybe they're exposing the mess you've been ignoring at home. Those "difficult" people are teachers in disguise. They're there to pull something out of you, to make you better—if you're humble enough to see it.

It is important that you know that grace is not weakness, nor is it letting stuff slide. Grace is giving people space to grow without letting them trample over you. When you operate from grace, you stop reacting to the drama and start leading the situation. That's what you call power—that's leadership hands down.

But don't think you can do all this without growing yourself. The second you think you've "arrived" is the second you start slipping. Leaders who stop learning, stop leading. Comfort zones are leadership killers. Steel sharpens steel. You've gotta stay hungry—hungry to learn, hungry to evolve, hungry to sharpen both your skills and your character.

Growth doesn't mean simply grabbing another title or collecting stripes. Growth happens when you actually become a better version of yourself. It's how you treat people when nobody's looking that's low-key integrity. It's how you handle the feedback that stings. It's how you stretch yourself even when it's uncomfortable. Your team will always reflect your growth. If you're stagnant, they'll be stagnant. If you're growing, they'll grow too.

And now is the time to think about legacy, because if all your leadership dies the day you walk out the door, what was it really worth? Legacy isn't about plaques or applause, but about people. It's not important what you leave *to* them—but what you leave *in* them. Did you open doors, and did you go back to bring people through? Did you hold the mic so tight that nobody else got to speak, or did you pass it and multiply your impact? Because real leaders don't just take up space—they make space.

This book isn't filled with quick hacks or sugarcoated tips. It guides you through doing the real work and understanding that leadership isn't about titles or applause—but making the kind of impact that ripples long after you've left the room.

As you turn these pages, don't just look for "leadership advice." Look for yourself. Where are you still pretending? Where do you need to set stronger boundaries? Where do you need to grow, stretch, or humble yourself? Where do you need to stop managing and start multiplying?

Because when it's all said and done, leadership is bigger than you. It speaks to the culture you create, the people you build, and the legacy you leave. Stay hungry. Stay grounded. Stay real. And above all, remember that your leadership will outlive your title if you do the work to make it count. Period.

"YOU TEACH PEOPLE HOW TO TREAT YOU EVERY TIME YOU CHOOSE SILENCE OR A STANDARD."

CHAPTER 1

WHAT'S YOUR *WHY*

Every leader has to know their "why." That's your anchor. It's what holds you steady when life gets chaotic and unpredictable. Challenges are going to come, but when you're grounded in your why, you've got the confidence to keep moving forward.

Let's get deep. Your why isn't just setting goals or stacking up accomplishments. It also involves *purpose*, or the deeper reason that drives you. I call this peeling back the onion. It checks whether your beliefs, your mindset, and your actions are truly in alignment.

Your why gives you that daily energy. It's what makes you show up with determination, especially when you're tired. It keeps you from bending and twisting into what society says you "should" be. And when you hit those moments where you feel like you can't take another step, your why kicks in and says, *You got this.*

I remember when I lost my grandmother—it was one of the hardest times of my life. But even through my grief, I knew I had to keep going. It was my why that reminded me of what mattered and why I started in the first place. And that gave me the strength to bounce back.

That's the gift of knowing and understanding your why. It's your built-in reminder of who you are and what's important. And when doubt tries to creep in your why speaks up, giving you the confidence to stand tall.

Commitment Can Be Challenged

Life—well, we know it be lifin'. One test after another will roll your way, and if you're not grounded, you'll be ready to toss in the towel at the first sign of trouble. That's what happens when someone hasn't figured out their "why." Without it, the path looks shaky, and every detour seems like an escape route. But when you know your why you're rooted. You're motivated. You stay the course even when the going gets rough.

Leaders, especially, must be crystal clear about who they are, what they bring to the table, and why they chose to step into that role. Frustration creeps in when failure seems to outweigh accomplishments. Your why silences all that noise and gives you clarity and the courage to keep moving with confidence.

It also sets the foundation for your own goals and can easily becomes a light for others. When you know who you are—your triggers, your motivators, your boundaries—you lead from a different place. And the people watching you take notes. They learn how to stand firm in uncertainty because you showed them how. That's true leadership.

The word *resilience* always comes to mind here. Your why keeps you aligned. It's the invisible cape that makes a team see their leader as a kind of superhero. When everything else is chaos, your people should trust that you'll be the one who brings clarity and direction.

Of course, the expectations of leadership don't always feel natural. Sometimes you'll have to go above and beyond in ways you didn't expect. But slow down for a minute and know that every extra commitment pulls from somewhere else in your life. You need to know the cost before you sign up.

Take me, for instance. I was one of three owners of my motorcycle club. Ownership kept me busy, sure, but when I decided to take on the Vice President role, whew—that was another level. Suddenly, I wasn't just meeting and planning with other owners. I was working with members, managing personalities, and being pulled away from home far more than I expected.

That's why I always advise new leaders to do their research. Talk to people who've walked the path before you. Get the details straight from the source so you know exactly what you're stepping into. Then, be honest about how the role will affect your lifestyle, your relationships, and your peace of mind. Share that with your loved ones too—because leadership doesn't happen in isolation.

At the end of the day, your why is both your commitment and your focus. In moments of doubt, when shortcomings feel bigger than strengths, your why brings you back to center. It reminds you of where you're headed and why it's worth it.

Think about physical fitness. Some people exercise for the look, others for the energy, and some because it's doctor's orders. Personally, when I discovered a serious health condition, working out stopped being optional—I needed it to survive. My why is simply -- I want to live. That's what gets me out of bed for a 5 in the morning workout, keeps me eating right, and ensures that I don't miss a doctor's appointments. My health is completely non-negotiable. These are the things that keep me disciplined and makes the goal attainable.

Never Compromise Your Values

I know firsthand how easy it is to start compromising your values when your foundation isn't steady. The pressure to bend to other people' expectations—or to play the game in environments that don't even share your values—can wear you down quick. That's another main reason why leaders need to know their why. Let me say it louder for the people in the back—it's your anchor!

We've heard it before: if you don't stand for something, you'll fall for anything right? And on this leadership journey, people will always have an opinion about what you *should and shouldn't* do. Their insight comes from their own story, their own upbringing—which may not look anything like yours. If you're not rooted in your why, you'll find yourself saying yes to things that don't even fit you, and before you know it, you're all the way off track.

Your values are your GPS. They guide you through tough decisions and keep you aligned with who you really are. That's why you have to be clear about your nonnegotiables—those hard lines you just don't cross. Let your no be no and stand on it. Some leaders struggle with being okay when people don't agree. Everybody won't clap for your choices. That's fine. If you know your decisions are ethical and in line with your values, keep it pushing.

We all know that leadership will test your backbone. You'll have moments where compromise looks easy, or where standing firm feels lonely. But don't let fear of judgment knock you off your square. Be willing to stand alone if you have to. You have to always stand ten toes down, because weak leadership gets walked over every single time.

And let's not pretend the pressures are always external. Sometimes you are the one tempting yourself to compromise. The money looks good. The title sounds impressive. The stability would help your family. Those are real factors. When you truly understand your why, you can tell the difference between alignment and distraction. That clarity gives you the strength to realign and keep moving forward without selling yourself short.

The world will always be loud—pressuring you to fit in, to do what "everybody else" is doing. If you're not clear on your values, you'll end up making moves that don't reflect who you really are. That's when people start feeling lost, disconnected, burnt out.

But when you stay rooted in your why you stop chasing approval and start leading with authenticity. You handle challenges with integrity. And no matter what's happening around you, you show up as the real you. And that's the kind of leadership people can trust.

We Are One

Knowing who you are sets the tone for how you connect with the people you lead. Knowing your values and being clear about your strengths and your weaknesses is the heartbeat of real leadership. I learned that understanding myself came before anything else. If I couldn't be real with me, how could I ever be real with anybody else?

Over time, I realized that my actions, decisions, and behaviors were all a reflection of what I believed deep down. Once I owned that, I could show up fully, and people could embrace the most genuine version of me—not some watered-down version.

It is evident that effective communication builds trust. When your team sees your real, non-fabricated self, they stop side-eyeing you. They don't see an imposter. They see a leader worth following. Respect grows when people know who you truly are. And being self-aware doesn't mean pretending to be perfect. It means owning your strengths and your blind spots.

Seriously—no leader has it all together. And it so important to understand that admitting where you're not strong doesn't make you weak—it makes you wise. It gives your team the chance to step up, to support you, and to strengthen the whole. Delegating with humility turns a personal weakness into a team win.

Life's journey is full of obstacles and curveballs. And you will never know how long each season is going to last or what it's going to demand of you. That's why it's so important to keep your why front and center. That's what inspires you to keep going, even when the road is rough.

Your why is the bridge between where you've been and where you're headed. Standing in the present, you can see how every piece of your story brought you here—and that understanding helps you lead with compassion. Because once you know your why, you start leading from purpose instead of ego.

When you stand tall in why you're here, your confidence becomes contagious. People connect to the genuine part of you, and they now can see and understand your vision. They understand the impact you're trying to make. And that's when leadership becomes a calling instead of a mere title.

TOOLS FOR SUCCESS

Alright, so let's talk about some tools that can really help you stay grounded in your why and show up as your best self in leadership. Think of these as your starter kit:

Self-Reflection Journals

Journaling is more than just writing—it's a mirror. Take time to jot down your thoughts, feelings, and what you're going through. When you're on edge or heated about a situation, grab that pen before you pop off. Write it out. Ask yourself: *What really happened? Could I have handled that differently?* And if that same situation comes back around, you can flip through your pages and say, "Ah, I've seen this before. Here's how I'm handling it this time." Journaling keeps you from making impulse moves that you'll regret later.

Personal Values Assessment (PVA)

This is basically an exercise to help you get crystal clear about your personal values. And don't just copy and paste what somebody else says matters—define it for yourself. Honesty, loyalty, commitment… these words mean different things to different people. I know for me, putting it in my own language is important. Once I've defined it, I hold to it. I don't bend just because somebody else's definition doesn't match mine.

This tool is about standing firm in *your* truth.

Books and Reflective Reading

You can't build strong leadership off memes and secondhand information. You've got to feed your own mind. Do your own reading, your own research. If you don't, you'll end up living life based on somebody else's opinions instead of your own. And if you feel too busy to sit down with a book, don't worry. Load up an audiobook for your commute. That ride from point A to point B will feel shorter, and you'll come out smarter on the other side.

And let me drop you a couple of good reads: *The Road Less Traveled* by M. Scott Peck and *Man's Search for Meaning* by Viktor Frankl. Both dig deep into purpose and self-discovery, and they'll challenge the way you see yourself and the world.

Life Coaching

Sometimes you need somebody outside your circle to help you sort through your thoughts and goals. A good life coach can ask the right questions, give you practical exercises, and help you clarify your identity, your values, and where you're headed. Don't be afraid to invest in that kind of support—it can take your growth to the next level.

At the end of the day, leadership is about knowing yourself, standing on your values, and leading from your why. That's the foundation. Without it, you'll get tossed around by opinions, pressures, and expectations that don't even belong to you. But when you're rooted you stand firm. You inspire confidence. And you create space for others to rise up and find their own why.

Don't forget—leadership is a journey, not a sprint. You're going to face challenges, seasons of doubt, and moments when quitting feels easier than pressing forward. That's natural. But it's in those moments where your why will push you to keep going.

So, lean into the tools. Journal it out. Define your values. Read and research for yourself. And if you need a coach or guide along the way, don't hesitate to get the help. Whatever you do, make sure every step you take aligns with the leader you're called to be.

Remember that you don't have to lead like anyone else. The world doesn't need a carbon copy—it needs the most authentic version of you. That's your power. That's your why. And that's what makes you a leader worth following.

REFLECTIONS

_____

_____

_____

_____

_____

_____

_____

_____

_____

_____

_____

_____

_____

_____

_____

_____

_____

_____

_____

_____

_____

_____

_____

_____

_____

_____

_____

_____

_____

_____

_____

_____

_____

_____

_____

_____

_____

_____

"MY TIME, MY ENERGY, MY PEACE—
THOSE ARE NOT OPEN-DOOR
POLICIES."

CHAPTER 2
ROOTS RUN DEEP

None of us started leading the day we got a title. Leadership starts way back—before the job, before the corner office, before the business card with your name on it. The way we were raised, the people who poured into us, the struggles we faced as kids... all of that runs deep and shapes how we show up as leaders today.

Some of us picked up positive traits early on—work ethic, resilience, discipline. Others may realize, *Whew, I got some habits I need to unlearn.* And that's okay. Great leaders don't pretend they've got it all figured out. They recognize their weak spots and commit to doing the inner work to grow.

Just because your past shaped you doesn't mean it defines you. At some point, you've got to decide if the character traits you're carrying line up with the morals and values you want to lead with. Your childhood might have been filled with lessons or with landmines—but both can teach you something if you're willing to look honestly.

For me, those early challenges became my training ground. They pushed me toward self-awareness, taught me how to communicate when silence felt easier, and sharpened my decision-making skills. The self-awareness I gained back then is still guiding me today, and it's what makes me show up as an authentic leader in both my personal and professional life.

Parental Influence on Leadership Style

The way we were raised has a whole lot to do with the way we lead. Whether we realize it or not, our parents—or whoever raised us—left fingerprints on our leadership style. Some of us grew up with parents who were natural mentors, pouring out wisdom and guidance. Others had homes filled with chaos, silence, or abandonment. Please understand that a tough childhood doesn't automatically mean you'll be a poor leader. What it does mean is you'll need to be honest with yourself, reflect, and be intentional about breaking patterns that don't serve you—or others for that matter.

Childhood is where we pick up mindsets, habits, and attitudes—good or bad—that follow us into adulthood. So, are you aware of which ones you're carrying? Are they really yours, or are you just repeating what you saw growing up? At some point, you've got to take inventory. Ask yourself: *The way I respond to stress, the way I handle conflict, the way I talk to people— where did I learn that? And do I actually want to keep it?*

I'll give you an example. In my house, communication was… let's just say it wasn't always pleasant. My mother and grandmother were strong women, true leaders in their own right. They ran things and what they said goes. But when it came to communication, their style was very direct and sometimes one-sided. Discussions easily turned into back and forth, and more often than not, someone shut down to avoid conflict. This could easily leave a person feeling like their voice didn't matter.

Now compare that to my friend Candace's household. When issues came up, her parents made space for real dialogue. They let her voice her perspective, and they listened. If things got heated, they'd step away, cool off, and then come back to the table when everybody was ready. That taught her that her voice had value. As an adult, you can see it in her leadership—she's supportive, transparent, and big on teamwork. She creates space for everyone on her team to contribute.

On the surface, Candace clearly had the advantage. My story didn't doom me. I could have chosen to lead based on my family's influence, but I made a different decision. I became intentional about breaking the cycle. Because I knew what it felt like to not have a voice, I now make sure my team always has one. I stay open to ideas, encourage input, and lean toward collaboration. My past gave me the empathy to lead differently—and that's a strength.

What I want you to take away is that your upbringing shaped you, but it doesn't define you. Reflect on how you were raised, yes. Be honest about both the strengths and the shortcomings you picked up along the way. But then—decide. Decide what stays and what goes. And don't be afraid to ask for feedback from your team as you grow. That willingness to reflect, adjust, and improve creates a positive and productive environment where everybody can thrive.

Know How You Lead

Understand that becoming a good, well-rounded leader takes work. It doesn't just fall into your lap. You've got to be intentional. There's no instruction manual. Leadership isn't "one size fits all." What works for me might not work for you. But if you know your values and you can see how they align with your life experiences, you're already on your way to being more effective.

Part of the process is observation and self-inventory—looking in the mirror and being honest about your leadership traits. But it's not just about self-reflection. You also have to be willing to listen to the people you lead. Feedback matters. You can't grow if you're always defensive or closed off. Be determined to find those areas where you need to level up, and then commit to doing the work. Let your team know your goals for growth and invite them to hold you accountable.

On a practical note, leadership lessons aren't only learned at work. You can learn just as much about yourself from how you show up at home or in your friendships. Think about it: when you plan a girls' trip, host a dinner, or pull together a bridal shower—how do you show up? Do you take charge in a way that empowers others, or do you bulldoze the process? Are you flexible when things don't go as planned, or does perfectionism have you spiraling? Are you listening to other perspectives, or are you lowkey ignoring the input of people around you? Those small, everyday moments can reveal a lot about your leadership style.

My friends don't hold back. If I'm being too pushy, they're quick to let me know. And I appreciate it. That kind of feedback keeps me grounded. In some ways, friends can hold you accountable even more than a team at work—because they're not worried about keeping a job, a paycheck, or a promotion. They'll check you because they love you, and that's real.

I also get feedback at home from my partner. He's told me before that I can be a little controlling. Now, my heart's desire is to make sure people feel valued and heard—so that feedback stung at first. But instead of shutting it down, I had to sit with it. I asked myself, *Is this true? Is this how I'm showing up?* Sometimes feedback won't match your intentions, but that doesn't mean it's wrong. The key is to listen with an open heart, take time to process it, and—if needed—get a second opinion from someone neutral who can see things from the outside.

At the end of the day, you don't have to accept every critique that comes your way. Not all feedback is constructive—some of it comes from people's own motives or frustrations. But if you filter it wisely, take in what's helpful, and show genuine understanding of others' perspectives, you'll grow stronger as a leader and build deeper trust with your team.

Leadership Styles Are Shaped by Experience

Tough times have a way of teaching us lessons you just can't learn in a classroom. Watching how strong leaders bounce back after setbacks gives the rest of us permission to keep pushing too. Now, not everybody has lived through major storms. Some people have been sheltered, never really tested. Others have lived what feels like battle after battle, barely coming up for air. When your back is against the wall, having a leader who's *been through something* makes a difference. They can empathize and speak from experience in a way that sparks hope.

In my first book, *Resilient AF: How to Fight for What You Deserve*, I shared my own story of growing up with my mom, without my dad in the picture. There were plenty of times I found myself in risky situations that could've cost me my future. But those experiences also shaped me. They taught me resilience. And that resilience became one of my greatest assets as a leader. Adversity doesn't just toughen you up—it gives you a strength and determination that equips you to guide others through their storms too.

There will be days in leadership when you'll want to quit. Days where you'll wonder, *Why am I even doing this? Who asked me to lead anyway?* You'll feel like the weight of the world is on your shoulders, and walking away will seem like the easier choice. I've been there. But overcoming the challenges of my past gave me the grit to endure. It gave me the ability to recognize when someone else is struggling and the courage to share my story so they know defeat isn't the only option.

If we're not careful, our hard times can leave us bitter. Past pain can show up as resentment, unfairness, or impatience in how we lead. That's why the real work starts with self-awareness. Ask yourself: *What prejudices have I developed from my past? How are they shaping the way I see and treat people now?* Once you identify them, you can start doing the work to heal.

And sometimes that healing requires professional help. Therapy doesn't mean you're weak. Talking it out, uncovering what's been tucked away, and learning new tools can help ensure your past doesn't leak into your leadership in ways you don't intend.

Good leaders reflect on their challenges instead of running from them. They use adaptability and problem-solving skills they've developed to show up stronger. And when you lead with that kind of transparency and strength, your team sees you not as someone who had it easy, but as someone who knows how to overcome. That kind of leadership inspires people to push past their own obstacles and rise.

Culture and Leadership

Culture shapes leadership. People come with their own ways of communicating, collaborating, and showing up, and as leaders, we can't afford to ignore that. I've traveled all over the country, and I've seen it firsthand—how people's values, their speech, even their whole approach to work is rooted in where they come from. That's why you've got to know who you're leading.

The reality is…not everyone is used to being heard. Some people have been conditioned to just keep quiet, take direction, and not rock the boat. They think silence equals acceptance. Silence usually hides frustration. People who feel invisible don't stay engaged for long—it eats away at them, and it hurts the team.

Take women raised in Middle Eastern cultures, for example. Because many of those societies are male-dominated, women may not feel comfortable speaking up in professional settings. That doesn't mean they don't have great ideas—it means they're not accustomed to having the freedom to share them. As a leader, you can't just shrug and say, "Well, they're quiet." No. You shift your approach. You call on them directly. You give them opportunities to step up. You make room at the table until they feel safe enough to take it. Inclusion is key.

For me, growing up Black in a deeply racist city in

Mississippi, the barriers looked different. My challenge wasn't about gender—it was about race. We weren't seen as leaders. We were seen as helpers, the ones expected to take orders, not give them. That reality forced me into a constant fight—to prove myself, to defend myself, to claim space that should've been mine in the first place. It made me tougher, yes, but it also made me defensive. That's baggage I had to unpack before I could lead effectively.

And I've seen other versions of this play out too. I once worked with someone who grew up in the system, without parents, without love. That kind of upbringing leaves scars. For them, trust was nearly impossible. They worked alone, kept their guard up, and carried a weight that most people couldn't see. People with that kind of background have so much potential, but they also have trauma to work through. As leaders, our job is to recognize that. To meet them where they are, to show compassion, and to help them grow without expecting them to be "perfect."

But there is a difference between empathy and favoritism. We can't only pour into the people who remind us of ourselves. Every team member deserves to be seen, heard, and supported. That means we have to lead fairly, even when it requires extra patience with some and a firmer push with others.

Everyone brings a perspective shaped by culture, upbringing, and previous experience. Good leadership means respecting those differences and creating an environment where they're not just tolerated but valued. It also means being honest when cultural norms clash with professional growth. Sometimes you'll need to challenge someone to stretch beyond what they're used to. Other times, you'll need to adjust your approach to create a safe space where they can thrive. It's a two-way street.

I know this firsthand because I've lived both sides. I know what it feels like to be silenced, and I know the freedom that comes when someone finally makes space for your voice. That's why I'm intentional about ensuring everyone on my

team is heard. Diversity and inclusion aren't buzzwords—
they're the foundation of strong, authentic leadership.

TOOLS FOR SUCCESS

Leadership Development Programs

Don't sleep on leadership programs. The good ones will call
out blind spots you didn't even know you had—like
unconscious bias—and push you to reflect on how you really
lead. They give you space to self-check, learn, and walk away
stronger.

Peer Networking and Learning

Get around other leaders. And not just people who look, talk,
and think like you—diverse voices matter. When you sit with
leaders from different backgrounds, you start to see your own
habits differently. They'll not only highlight areas where you
can improve, but also affirm the things you're doing right so
you can stay consistent. Trust me, you'll leave those
conversations with new tools, new perspectives, and a broader
way of thinking.

Coaching and Mentorship

I'll say it plain: every leader needs guidance. Coaches, mentors,
therapists—they're all valuable in different ways. Personally, I
believe God, therapy, and coaching are the holy trinity of good
leadership. A spiritual teacher gives you direction and clarity.
A therapist helps you deal with the baggage—those cultural
and childhood wounds that creep into how you lead. And a
coach? Whew. My coach is like a talking journal. I can unpack
situations, look at them from another angle, and get clarity on
why people act the way they do. It's perspective I can't always
get on my own.

360-Degree Feedback

Want the real tea on how you're doing? Don't just look up to your boss for reviews—get feedback from every angle: your peers, your team, and your higher-ups. That's called 360-degree feedback. It can be formal—through surveys or reviews—or informal, like adding an anonymous suggestion box in the office. Either way, you'll get honest insight into how people actually experience your leadership.

Regular Team Check-Ins

Finally, set a rhythm with your team. Weekly or bi-weekly check-ins keep everybody connected and give people space to voice concerns before they turn into problems. Make it a safe space. When your team knows they can speak freely, they'll trust you more—and that trust will turn into better collaboration and a stronger team culture.

At the end of the day, tools are only as powerful as your willingness to use them. Leadership development programs, coaches, mentors, check-ins, feedback—all of it is meant to sharpen you, not shame you. The real win comes when you approach these practices with honesty, humility, and a desire to grow.

Remember, your why is your anchor. These tools are just the chisels that help shape you into the kind of leader your team can trust. So don't just collect information—apply it. Stay open, stay teachable, and never be afraid to look in the mirror. Because the leader you're becoming will always be more important than the leader you've been.

REFLECTIONS

_____

_____

_____

_____

_____

_____

_____

_____

_____

_____

_____

_____

_____

_____

_____

_____

_____

_____

_____

_____

_____

_____

_____

_____

_____

_____

_____

_____

_____

_____

_____

_____

_____

_____

_____

_____

_____

_____

_____

_____

_____

_____

_____

_____

_____

_____

_____

_____

_____

_____

_____

_____

_____

_____

_____

_____

"A MINDFUL LEADER DOESN'T CHASE CONTROL. THEY PRACTICE SELF-CONTROL."

CHAPTER 3
MIRROR TALK

Growth-minded leaders understand something crucial: their leadership leaves a mark. Whether they realize it or not, their impact shows up in the way their team moves and how people feel about working with them. A good leader knows this and pays attention. They take note of where their influence shows up—and then they get intentional about using strategies to make sure their impact is positive.

Impact is simply the mark you make on others. It can be positive, neutral, or negative—and all three tell a story. A positive impact lights a fire in people. It makes them want to show up, do better, and even rise into leadership themselves. On the flip side, when leadership sucks (to be brutally honest), it drags down performance and leaves people questioning if they even want to be here. Sometimes bad leadership pushes people to do better by making sure *they* don't repeat those mistakes. I know I became a better leader after experiencing the fallout of others' poor leadership. But I don't recommend it. The goal should never be to make your team learn resilience from surviving you.

This is something very important to understand. Neutral impact is just as dangerous. That's when you're a placeholder—going through the motions, checking boxes, not growing but not folding either. The problem is, no one remembers neutral leaders. They don't leave legacies, they don't move the needle, and eventually, the team stalls out. Leadership should never be about settling.

So, if you want to lead well, start by looking at your reflection—not just in the mirror, but in your team. Are they showing up on time? Focused? Producing results without you constantly breathing down their necks? That's your influence at work. Or are they slacking, avoiding you when problems arise? That's also your influence. Whether you like it or not, your team is a reflection of you.

Although uncomfortable, as a leader, you've got to take accountability. If your team is struggling, you don't get to just point fingers. Leadership means owning it. If you're not willing to admit where you've fallen short, maybe leadership isn't the right seat for you. But if you can face it honestly—if you can say, "There's room for me to grow"—then you're already on the right track.

I had to learn this myself. Over 25 years in the military, I transitioned into leading more in civilian organizations. I remained active in the service as well. And whew—let me tell you, that was an adjustment. In the military, my direct, sharp tone was normal. In my mind, I was respectful. But in a civilian office that same tone came across as aggressive, even rude. I didn't mean to be that way, but intention doesn't erase impact. That lesson taught me something powerful: it's not just *what* you communicate, it's *how*.

Being mindful of your tone, your delivery, and your character traits is key to understanding your leadership style. Some people pride themselves on being "straight to the point" or "black and white," but what works in one circle doesn't always work in another. Your friends might let you get away with bluntness, but your team might find it abrasive. That gap can damage relationships if you're not paying attention.

I had to face that gap in my personal life too. Even at restaurants, I'd place my order so directly that it rubbed servers the wrong way. I wasn't trying to be rude—I just wanted to be clear. But feedback made me realize that my delivery was off-putting, and that mattered. Leadership doesn't stop when you clock out. How you carry yourself in one space eventually seeps into every space.

Knowing how to show up—when to soften your tone, when to stand firm, when to listen—is at the heart of effective leadership. And the only way to grow here is to invite feedback. Don't get offended when people call you out. Reflect on it, filter through it, and decide where you need to adjust. Pair that with empathy and active listening, and you'll bridge the communication gaps that hold so many leaders back.

Because real leadership is not about barking orders. It's about creating an environment where people feel valued, understood, and motivated to give their best.

The Ripple Effect of Your Actions

How people view you impacts your whole team. The way you show up, the way you respond to things—it's all being watched. If you're late all the time, don't expect your team to respect deadlines. If you want better communication but you're closed off, don't expect people to magically open up. And if you cut corners or act unethically, trust me—they'll pick up on it, whether you realize it or not. Understand that leaders set the tone. If you want your team to do right, you've got to lead by example.

Let me tell you about one of the most unforgettable team meetings I've ever sat through. We were supposed to be hashing out a few issues, but our leader came in hot. He had already been venting in earlier meetings about his boss—way too comfortable with us, crossing boundaries he shouldn't have crossed. That day, his frustration boiled over. In the middle of the discussion, he lost it—flipped a desk, papers flying everywhere, like a bomb had gone off in the room.

We were frozen. Nobody moved. Nobody knew if it was

about to get worse. In that moment, it wasn't about the desk or the papers—it was about how unsafe we suddenly felt. From then on, the energy shifted completely. Instead of focusing on solutions, we were focused on survival—getting through the day without setting him off again.

One outburst wrecked everything. Trust was gone. We stopped speaking up, stopped sharing ideas, stopped engaging. We were walking on eggshells, worried another explosion was around the corner. Eventually, he was fired, but the damage didn't leave with him. When a new leader stepped in, the team was already shut down. We didn't trust the replacement, even though they hadn't done anything wrong. That one man's behavior created a ripple effect that stained the entire organization.

That experience taught me something I'll never forget, which is that leaders set the emotional climate. When you lose control, it doesn't just impact the moment—it lingers. It changes how people see you, how they see the company, and how safe they feel showing up to work.

So how do you prevent that? Emotional awareness. Start with yourself. Know your triggers. Pay attention to the moments where you feel yourself heating up and learn when to step back. If you get bad news or you're in a tense situation, take a pause. Walk away if you have to. Most anger comes from miscommunication or limited perspective, so ask yourself: *Am I missing something?*

Don't answer questions or confront people while you're still on fire. The moment you lose your temper, you lose your power. Rebuilding that trust is ten times harder than excusing yourself and returning later. Take that time to breathe, pray, journal, or talk it through with a trusted advisor. Then come back to the table calm and clear-headed.

Every decision you make, every reaction you show, ripples outward. It doesn't just hit your team—it can affect your whole organization and even the larger community around you. That's why self-control isn't just about keeping your cool—it's about protecting your influence. A mindful, composed leader creates safety. And safety is what allows teams to thrive.

Leadership Blind Spots

It's time to start doing the intentional work to fix our blind spots. Understand that blind spots are tricky. You don't know what you don't know. (Read that again.) That's why self-awareness is key. It takes reflection *and* honest feedback from the people around you to even see them.

A blind spot can look like a lot of things. Maybe you're afraid to ask for help. Maybe you care a little too much about how people see you. Or maybe you've got that "know it all" vibe that shuts out the wisdom of others. Sometimes it's dodging tough conversations, pointing fingers instead of taking accountability, or working so much that your family barely sees you. The problem with blind spots is that most of us don't realize we have them until somebody points them out.

Here's an example: if you struggle with time management, chances are you're not just wasting your own time—you're wasting everybody else's too. And you may not even notice it. But when someone finally calls it out, that's your cue. That's your chance to say, *Okay, I see it now. Let me do better.*

I can recognize blind spots in others now because I've learned to find my own. But I wasn't always this self-aware. As an only child, I was set in my ways—selfish even. At home, that showed up in the way I made decisions with my partner. It took some uncomfortable conversations (and yes, some hard feedback) to realize how much my behavior was impacting him. My first instinct was to get defensive. But defensiveness kept me stuck. Once I dropped that guard and started listening, I grew.

Even in small group settings, like deciding where to eat, the old me would push hard for my choice. I had to practice letting go, being cooperative, and listening to what other people wanted. That taught me that leadership is about humility. It's about being self-aware, flexible, and open to growth.

You need to know that not all feedback is created equal. Sometimes people project their own stuff onto you. They'll try to mold you into who they want you to be, not who you actually are. A strong-willed woman, for example, can be mislabeled just because the people around her are passive. So here's the rule—check the source. Ask yourself: *Is this feedback about me, or is it about them?*

Take me for instance. I've had people tell me I don't smile enough. "Why do you always look so serious?" they ask. That made me pause and reflect. Am I rude? Am I disrespectful? No. Then maybe what they're feeling is their own discomfort with my serious face. If I'm not harming anyone, then forcing myself to smile just to make them comfortable would mean shrinking into their little box. And that's not happening.

Here's how you check: if your behavior is negatively affecting your team, you owe it to them to do the work and change it. But if it's just about someone else's preference, be careful not to compromise your authenticity for their comfort. Leadership isn't about appeasing everyone—it's about showing up as your true self, with integrity and awareness.

So, take a moment to reflect. Look at how you lead at home, at work, and in your community. How do your actions impact those around you? And when feedback comes, don't get defensive. Listen. Filter. Decide what's valid and what's not. Because the leader who leans into feedback with humility and openness is the leader who grows into empathy, authenticity, and strength.

TOOLS FOR SUCCESS

Active Listening

One of the most powerful tools in leadership—and in life—is knowing how to really listen. And I don't mean listening just to clap back or defend yourself. I mean listening to *understand*. When you quiet down, you can usually hear the root of the issue. But if you're always gearing up for a defense, you'll miss it every time.

The challenge is staying quiet when emotions are high. But if you can pause long enough to hear someone out—their frustration, their explanation—you can respond with clarity instead of reacting from a place of hurt or ego.

For example, let's say your partner keeps complaining that you're "too busy." Now, you know you spend plenty of time together, so on the surface, their complaint doesn't add up. But if you lean in and listen, you may realize the root issue isn't about your schedule at all—it's about past wounds, old expectations, or unhealthy attachments that predate your relationship. Listening with empathy lets you see the real problem and break cycles that arguments alone can't fix.

Performance Reviews (Done Right)

Now, let's talk about your team. Regular one-on-one check-ins aren't just about critiquing their work. They're also a chance to check your own temperature as a leader. These conversations should be safe spaces where you *both* bring your concerns to the table.

Here's one of my favorite questions to ask: *"How can I better support you in your role?"* That one question opens the door for feedback without putting them on the spot. If they say, "I could use more feedback," that might mean you're not communicating as clearly as you think. If they say, "I could use more encouragement," maybe you need to do more to build a culture of motivation and recognition.

Don't go in asking, "Do you think I'm an effective leader?" Nobody is going to risk their job by saying no. Instead, ask open-ended questions that give you insight without making them feel attacked. Try:

- *"Describe a perfect day in your position."* Their answer may reveal things you didn't see. ("A perfect day is one where I can take my lunch on time." Translation:

you've been ignoring the need for breaks.)

- *"What's working well for you right now?"* Start positive so they don't feel defensive.

- *"What's not working so well for you?"* This gives space for constructive honesty.

- *"How can I better show up for you as a leader?"* This ties it all back to your role and responsibility.

When you ask the right questions, you don't just measure their performance—you measure your own impact as a leader. And that's where growth really happens.

Leadership isn't about titles, paychecks, or corner offices—it's about impact. Every word you speak, every decision you make, every way you show up leaves an imprint on the people around you. The question is: what kind of impact are you leaving?

Your team is a mirror. Their energy, their performance, even their silence reflects back the kind of leader you are. If you don't like what you see, it's not the time for excuses—it's the time for accountability. That's where growth begins.

Being a leader means being willing to face your blind spots, to receive feedback without getting defensive, and to adapt when your style is doing more harm than good. It means listening more than you speak, leading with compassion, and knowing when to stand firm in your authenticity—even if it makes people uncomfortable.

Yes, the work is hard. Yes, it requires humility. But the good news is that the more intentional you are about growing, the more effective you become—not just for your team, but for yourself. Because real leadership isn't about perfection. It's about progress. It's about choosing every day to show up better than you did the day before.

So as you move forward, remember this: your leadership

has the power to build or to break, to inspire or to discourage, to silence or to amplify. Choose wisely. Do the work. And never forget that the most influential leaders are the ones who lead with awareness, integrity, and heart.

REFLECTIONS

_____

_____

_____

_____

_____

_____

_____

_____

_____

_____

_____

_____

_____

_____

_____

_____

_____

_____

_____

_____

_____

_____

_____

_____

_____

_____

_____

_____

_____

_____

_____

_____

_____

_____

_____

_____

_____

_____

_____

_____

"IF THE ROOM COSTS YOU YOUR VOICE, IT'S TOO EXPENSIVE."

CHAPTER 4
KEEP IT REAL

Time out for pretending. Leadership isn't some mask you pull out the closet when you feel like playing "grown up." Real leadership—world-class leadership—comes from the heart. It's about staying grounded, staying approachable, and being the kind of person people *want* to follow, not because of your title, but because they believe in you.

Let's break that down.

Stay Grounded Being grounded means never forgetting where you come from. It's about humility. Yes, growth is beautiful—celebrate it—but don't let it puff you up with pride and ego. The minute you start looking down on people, you've already failed as a leader. Remember your own beginnings. Remember the times you needed grace. And then extend that same grace to others.

Be Approachable Gucci shoes or not, you better still be approachable. (Yeah, I said it.) If your team can't come to you when something's wrong, you've already lost half the battle. Be a safe space—period. When leaders shut people out, they don't stop talking; they just stop talking to *you*. And when frustrations only get vented sideways in break rooms or group chats, chaos brews, morale drops, and nothing gets resolved. Keep the door open, keep your ears open, and make sure your people know they can bring the real to you.

Lead with Authenticity Authenticity is everything. Fake energy is loud, and people will pick up on it faster than you think. An inauthentic leader creates distance, mistrust, and tension in the workplace. Professionalism is the baseline— that's the bare minimum. What separates a good leader is truth and sincerity. If all you're giving your team is surface-level small talk—"hi" and "bye"—don't expect deep connection or loyalty. Real leadership requires real connection.

Respect Over Fear Every leader at some point asks themselves: *Do I want to be respected or feared?* If you're grounded and humble, you'll choose respect every time. Fear may get people to follow orders in the short term, but it doesn't build trust, loyalty, or longevity. Fear creates eggshells. It makes people do just enough to avoid punishment while secretly resenting you the whole time. And resentment spreads like wildfire.

Respect, on the other hand, hits different. Respect builds unity. It creates a culture where people believe in you and in what you're building together. When your team trusts your judgment and values your character, they'll go above and beyond—not out of fear, but because they're riding with you.

This may be news to some, but respect isn't instant. You don't walk into a room and automatically have it. It's built over time, through consistency, character, and care. But once it's there it doesn't just stop at the office door. Respect has a way of carrying beyond company walls, creating long-term relationships that last well past the job.

Emotional Intelligence is Your Leadership Superpower

Keeping it all the way 100—emotional intelligence is the

real key to leading like a boss. It's about knowing your own emotions and checking them *before they check you*. At the same time, it's being able to read the room, sense how others are feeling, and respond in ways that build them up instead of breaking them down. Leaders who practice this don't just run teams—they create communities where people feel valued, respected, and seen.

A big piece of emotional intelligence is staying tuned in to what's happening inside of you. If you're sad, frustrated, or annoyed, pay attention to that before it spills over into the workplace. Because whether you realize it or not, your personal energy sets the tone.

Let me give you an example. I've had times where a superior projected her frustration onto me after tension had already been building. I've even been guilty of doing the same thing myself in the past—letting stress roll downhill onto somebody else. It doesn't benefit anybody. That kind of negative energy doesn't solve the problem. It teaches the wrong lesson, which is how *not* to manage emotions.

What builds trust is the opposite: staying calm and level-headed even under pressure. When your team knows you won't lose it, they feel safe. They can focus on the mission instead of bracing for your mood swings. Because it's hard—nearly impossible—to trust a leader whose emotions are all over the place.

And while yes, we're all human, leaders don't get the luxury of dumping their frustrations onto the people they lead. That's how resentment builds. That's how "Negative Nancy" is born in the workplace—the person who walks in every day carrying drama, attitude, or burdens from outside the office. Sometimes, her bad vibe has nothing to do with you at all. That's why grace is important. But grace doesn't mean tolerance for toxic energy. A good leader has compassion while still setting boundaries. Sometimes that means saying, *"Look, I understand you're going through it, but I need you to check that at the door—or the car—before you step into this space."*

Emotional intelligence doesn't mean ignoring emotions; it means managing them with wisdom. It means creating a culture where even when life outside is heavy, people know they can step into a safe, steady environment at work.

Draw the Personal-Professional Line

Most professionals juggle more than just work. We all have personal lives—families, relationships, struggles—that can easily spill into the workplace if we're not careful. And this is where emotional intelligence really gets tested.

I've had times when tension at home made it hard to show up fully for my team. If I felt misunderstood in my relationship, that energy wanted to follow me into meetings, phone calls, even casual conversations with clients. My team didn't deserve to carry the weight of what I was going through. That's when I had to stretch myself—to separate my emotions, release what I was feeling, and choose to show up for them instead of projecting my personal frustrations onto the people I lead.

For me, it felt like the separation of church and state. My personal emotions stayed at the door. Period. Because the moment you lose control in one setting, it bleeds into every other role you hold. The people closest to you—the ones you love—often have the most power to throw you off balance. If you're not careful, that imbalance will show up at work and undermine your leadership.

What helped me was letting go of control. I had to accept that I couldn't fix everything in my personal life before I walked into the office. Until I did that, compartmentalizing was essential. I had to draw a line: personal struggles on one side, professional responsibilities on the other.

Now, don't get me wrong—this isn't about being fake. It's about being strong and strategic enough to manage your emotions so they don't manage you. It's about showing up authentically when it's time to lead, without letting yesterday's argument or last night's frustration dictate how you treat people today.

Use a Filter, Period

The transfer of energy is real, so you've got to guard your space. Think about it—when you're dealing with something heavy and you confide in another leader or a friend, you're opening yourself up to their perspective. And not all advice deserves a seat at your table. That's why emotional intelligence also means knowing how to filter what you hear. Take what's useful, and respectfully toss the rest.

Not all advice comes from a pure place. Sometimes people speak out of their own pain, frustration, or unhealed experiences. If you're not discerning, you can end up carrying their baggage right on top of your own.

If you're struggling in your relationship, would you really call up a friend who's been through nothing but toxic romances for advice? Hopefully not. Because unless they've done their healing, their words may reflect their wounds, not wisdom. Instead of giving you clarity, they might just hand you their bitterness.

That's why it's so important to be selective about who you confide in. This isn't personal—it's protection. People can mean well and still give you advice that's clouded by bias, pain, or old trauma. As you grow in emotional intelligence, you'll start to recognize the difference. You'll learn which voices bring clarity and which ones bring confusion.

The key is to nurture your connections enough to know people's history, their patterns, and their perspective. That way, you'll know who to go to for level-headed, sincere guidance—and who you might love dearly but can't trust with certain conversations. Because protecting your energy is just as important as protecting your time.

Focus on Solutions

A friend of mine once shared a story about when she was teaching high school. She was pregnant at the time— hormones and emotions all over the place—and she was preparing to lead 500 people at a school event. Stress was high, money and resources were low (public school problems, you know how that goes), and vendors were flaking left and right.

She finally went to her principal, her boss, and just let it all out—venting nonstop for a full two minutes about everything that was going wrong. The principal didn't interrupt. She didn't roll her eyes. She just listened. And when my friend finally came up for air, the principal calmly said, *"Go to the office and tell them to let you use sponsor money."* Then she walked away, cool as ever.

That moment stuck with my friend. The principal didn't coddle her with "poor you" talk, and she didn't scold her for being emotional. She simply listened, and then offered a clear solution. That's emotional intelligence in action—knowing that half the battle is letting people be heard. Listening itself is a form of empathy. The solution comes after.

But there was another layer. The principal's calm response made my friend reflect on how she had handled the situation. Instead of shaming her, the principal modeled composure and professionalism—traits my friend realized she wanted for herself. That's what "leading by example" looks like. Respond, don't react. Model the behavior you want to see in others.

Watch For Shifts

Emotional intelligence isn't just about managing your own emotions—it's also about noticing shifts in others.

When I was serving as a First Sergeant instructor, graduation day for the troops was a huge deal. We'd taken them through hell—broken them down to build them back up—and finishing the process was no small feat. Families usually came to cheer them on, but sometimes, due to distance or circumstance, loved ones couldn't make it. And you could see the difference. The smiles didn't quite reach their eyes. Heads hung lower. Energy dipped.

As a leader, I couldn't just ignore that shift. I pulled my fellow instructors aside and said, *"Listen, we've got to make sure every single troop feels celebrated—family present or not."* We got creative. We set up a virtual option so families could watch live from anywhere. I'll never forget telling one troop, whose family wasn't there, *"They're watching you right now, and they're proud of you—just like I am."* The way their face lit up? Priceless.

We also invited other chiefs to attend and cheer, even if they didn't have graduates in the class. The message was clear: *You are not alone. We are your family too.*

Those small shifts made a huge impact. It wasn't just about boosting morale—it was about reminding them that leadership sees them, values them, and has their back. That's the heart of emotional intelligence: paying attention to the quiet signals and stepping in to turn someone's disappointment into encouragement.

Empathy May Solve Conflicts, But Can't Always Save You

Conflict has a way of defining you as a leader. Most conflicts are really opportunities for growth—if you approach them with empathy. You must know that empathy is not weakness. It's not about being "soft." Empathy is a superpower, just like emotional intelligence. It's about stepping into someone else's shoes, understanding their perspective—even if you don't agree—and showing that you care. You don't always have to fix the problem. Sometimes just recognizing someone's feelings takes the edge off and opens the door for real dialogue.

When empathy is embedded in leadership, the whole focus shifts to the team. You pay attention. You listen to understand, not just to respond. That builds connection. But please know that too much empathy without boundaries can weaken your position. Work is not group therapy, and endless pats on the back don't keep a business moving. A good leader knows how to empathize without losing order, because respect still matters. The healthiest workplaces value people *and* productivity.

Let me share a moment that stretched me. When I hosted my third annual conference, I thought my past experience had me fully prepared. I had a full team—event planners, designers, vendors—the works. Everything was smooth until the week before the event, when my decorator lost her father. This was her second year working with me, and I was used to her strong communication, but after her father's passing, I barely heard from her at the most critical time.

I understood she was grieving, but I was also overwhelmed with the weight of this event—people were traveling from all over the country. Mentally, emotionally, and financially, I was all in. But I was frustrated. I checked in, tried to be empathetic, but when she finally showed up the night before—late and still overcome with grief—it threw everything off balance. Truth be told, it just killed the vibe—and rightfully so.

I wanted to be compassionate, but I also needed her to show up for me and the event. In the chaos of preparation, my emotions got the best of me. I walked away, and later heard she broke down in tears. The next day, I stood before my guests composed, but inside I was shaken. The hardest part was that I believed I had shown empathy, but she didn't see it that way. From her perspective, I failed her.

Looking back, I can admit I was in "business mode," and she was in "heartbroken mode." Those two worlds didn't meet. She stretched herself, hoping her effort would be enough, and I needed more than she could give. In hindsight, the most compassionate thing I could've done was release her—offer condolences, thank her, and maybe invite her back the next year. But in the moment, I couldn't see that.

This is the reality of leadership. Sometimes empathy and execution collide. Sometimes your best intentions will be misunderstood. And sometimes you'll realize too late that both sides were expecting something the other couldn't deliver.

The lesson? Emotional intelligence won't erase conflict, but it will help you manage it better. It helps you make tough calls with compassion, minimize damage, and recognize when a situation simply isn't workable. Because real leadership means owning the tension between caring for people and carrying the mission—and knowing when to prioritize one without destroying the other.

Start with Self-Awareness & Checking Yourself

You cannot lead others if you're not checking in with yourself. Take at least a minute every day to pause and ask: *How am I really feeling today? And how might this come across to the people I encounter?*

Your team can feel your energy—good or bad. You don't have to be perfect, and you can still lead on your off days, but you do need to be intentional. Acknowledging, *"I'm not my usual self today,"* can help you communicate better and keep what you're feeling from spilling over into how you lead.

Pay Attention to the Team

You're not a mind reader, but leaders have to pay attention. Notice body language, tone, and shifts in mood. Don't ignore the energy in the room. If something feels off, lean into it—don't wait for tension to explode later.

This may feel heavy, but suicide is real. Sometimes the smallest signs are signals that someone needs help. Your awareness could literally make the difference between life and death.

Respond, Don't React

Woosah! Good leaders stay poised, no matter what. Reacting in anger, snapping back, or losing your cool never helps—it only escalates the problem. The more unbothered and in control you are under pressure, the more peace your team will have.

Remember this: when people feel powerless, they tend to react. But leaders aren't called to react; leaders are called to *respond*. Stay calm, collected, and always remember your power.

Celebrate Small Wins

Don't wait for major milestones to celebrate your team.

Acknowledge the small things too. Those little wins build confidence, trust, and momentum.

Many people downplay their contributions because they're not used to being celebrated—or even celebrating themselves. A leader who notices and affirms the "small stuff" builds loyalty and helps the team believe in themselves.

Trust Starts with Keeping It 100

Authenticity and transparency aren't extras—they're the foundation of trust. People don't connect with perfection; they connect with honesty. Your ability to admit mistakes, share struggles, and show up authentically will do more for your leadership than trying to appear flawless ever will.

For a long time, I was extremely private. I kept my health struggles hidden because I didn't want to look weak. I thought strong leadership meant never crying, never admitting pain, and holding it all together no matter what. But I was falling apart inside. Vertigo, fatigue, medication side effects—I was dragging myself to work pretending like everything was fine.

One day, in the middle of a coaching session, a client told me, *"You just don't get it. You never struggle, so you can't possibly understand."* That moment shook me. I realized my silence was creating distance. I wasn't connecting because I wasn't letting anyone see the real me.

So, I tried something new. I opened up. I admitted that I had been struggling just to show up, that some days I didn't feel strong enough to keep going—but I kept pushing because my purpose was bigger than my pain. And in that moment, everything shifted. My client's guard dropped. She began to trust me on a deeper level. From that day forward, our relationship—and the way I led—completely changed.

When I stopped pretending and started keeping it real, my clients trusted me more, not less. They shared more, leaned in more, and felt freer to be honest about their own struggles. I learned that vulnerability is a two-way street. Real strength isn't in hiding pain; it's in admitting you're human and still choosing to press forward.

Don't get me wrong: authenticity doesn't mean oversharing. Boundaries matter. Share enough to connect, not to unload. Talking about your health challenges may build trust; talking about sexual fetishes, for example, would cross professional lines and make people uncomfortable, and...*eww*. As a leader, you get to decide what's appropriate for the space and the relationship. Sometimes peer-to-peer conversations invite deeper sharing. And sometimes, in a leadership role, just a little vulnerability is enough to build relatability.

The goal isn't to bare it all—it's to keep it real. Show your humanity, maintain your boundaries, and lead with honesty. That's how you build trust that lasts.

TOOLS FOR SUCCESS

Nobody Likes a Perfect Patty

Don't front like everything is perfect when it's not—that's a rookie move. If you're having an off day, be honest about it. Share your struggles and invite your team to help brainstorm solutions. That kind of transparency builds trust, and it reminds everyone that you're all in this together.

Own Your Mistakes

This is one of my non-negotiables. When I mess up, I own it. No excuses, no finger-pointing. And I expect the same from others. Excuses erode trust, but accountability earns respect. The moment you admit your fault and take responsibility, your team will see you as a stronger, not weaker, leader.

You're Human, Right?

Don't be afraid of your humanity—and don't forget to recognize it in others. When someone slips up, I remind myself: *they're human, just like me.* We all misinterpret, overlook, or drop the ball sometimes. A little grace goes a long way.

And let's not forget—your people are your most valuable asset. Even in high-demand settings like the military, the mission can't overshadow connection. Slow down. Ask about your team's lives beyond the workplace. Tap into what makes them tick. You'll be amazed how much stronger your bond becomes.

Create Safe Spaces

People can't thrive where they don't feel safe. One of my associates works at a company with a strict "anti-gossip" policy—messy talk could cost you your job. But her director balances that by hosting quarterly check-ins. Each employee has the chance to name someone they enjoy working with and someone they'd rather not partner with. No judgment, no backlash—just honesty in a structured, safe environment.

That's the key: a safe space isn't about venting for the sake of drama. It's about creating clarity, preventing confusion, and helping your team feel heard. Build an environment where your people know they can speak truth without fear, judgment, or retaliation.

Leadership is not about putting on a mask and pretending to have it all together. Nobody's buying that. And honestly—nobody wants that. People don't connect with "perfect." They connect with *real*.

When you're willing to own your mistakes, admit when you're struggling, and keep it 100 with your team, you show them that you're human. And that humanity is what earns their trust. They'll follow you not just because you're the boss, but because they believe you care, they believe in your vision, and they believe you're willing to walk through the fire with them.

At the end of the day, leading with heart doesn't make you soft—it makes you strong. It creates teams that will grind for you, stand by you, and celebrate with you, because they know you're not just in charge… you're *in it* with them.

So stop chasing perfection. Show up, be present, be real.

That's the kind of leadership people remember—and the kind they'll ride for.

REFLECTIONS

_____

_____

_____

_____

_____

_____

_____

_____

_____

_____

_____

_____

_____

_____

_____

_____

_____

_____

_____

_____

_____

_____

_____

_____

_____

_____

_____

_____

_____

_____

_____

_____

_____

_____

_____

_____

_____

_____

_____

_____

"GROWTH REQUIRES TWO THINGS: HONEST SELF-REFLECTION AND UNAPOLOGETIC BOUNDARIES."

CHAPTER 5
FLIP THE SCRIPT ON CONFLICT

Everybody knows what it feels like when tension creeps into the room. People aren't seeing eye to eye, voices get sharp, and suddenly everything feels like sandpaper. Conflict isn't the end of the world. It doesn't have to tear your team apart. If you handle it right, it can actually pull people closer, build trust, and make the whole team stronger.

Now, if I can speak freely—the current political and economic climate in America got everybody on edge. No office is immune to it, and no citizen can avoid it. And in 2025, with government shake-ups and workplaces under pressure to justify roles while diversity and inclusion practices get stripped away, fear is running rampant. Meetings that used to be quick and clean are now running long, emotions are high, and people are losing their cool. Some days, I can't decide if I need popcorn, a Kleenex, or a quick prayer just to get through it.

But as leaders, that's when the weight falls on us. People are worried about their livelihoods, about changes they can't control. And that's when our ability to handle conflict gets tested the most.

What I've learned is that conflict isn't really about the yelling, the silence, or the slammed doors. Simply, conflict is failed communication or a lack of understanding. Sometimes it's the loud voice that *has* to win every argument. Sometimes it's the quiet team member who checks out, shows up late, or mutters "that's above my pay grade" before tuning out completely. Both are signs that conflict is being mishandled. And if left unchecked, they infect the team like a slow-growing cancer.

Understand that conflict isn't always bad. In fact, it can be the very thing that helps a group grow, if you know how to frame it. Healthy conflict pushes people to really listen, to practice empathy, and to find solutions that make the team better. It doesn't have to be about blame, winners, or losers. It can be about progress.

At the end of the day, most people just want two things: to be heard and to be respected. When they feel overlooked, undervalued, or dismissed, they react the way they've been conditioned—lashing out, shutting down, or letting ego take the wheel. And while therapy (good therapy, not Instagram memes) can help people unpack their personal stuff, you don't need a psychology degree to manage conflict well.

You just need to remember that conflict isn't a threat—it's an opportunity. It's not "if" but *when*. And the leaders who try to avoid it, run from it, or act like it doesn't exist miss out on one of the greatest tools for growth. Conflict forces us to face uncomfortable truths, deal with the issues we'd rather dodge like bullets, and strengthen relationships by pushing through the hard stuff together.

When you stop seeing conflict as the enemy and start seeing it as the training ground for deeper trust and stronger teams, you're not just surviving—you're evolving. That's when what looks like a setback becomes a win.

Be Bullet Proof

At the top of 2025, one executive order rocked the workplace—the removal of Diversity, Equity, and Inclusion (DEI) from countless organizations. For over 60 years, DEI opened doors, shaped opportunities, and created pathways for minorities and underrepresented groups. Now that it's gone, people are starting to feel the difference, and not in a good way.

As a leader, you can't control that. You're not writing the policies—you're just tasked with carrying them out. When people's jobs and livelihoods are on the line, leaders often become the punching bag. People know you're "just the messenger," but when rent is due and bills don't stop, emotions take over—and that bullet I referenced earlier—yeah, you're now the bullseye.

That's why you've got to be bullet proof. Don't take it personally. Communicate clearly. And let people have space to process their feelings without jumping into debates. Politics don't belong in the workplace—you stick to the task at hand.

Being professional doesn't mean being cold. You can empathize, you can listen, you can even offer support like a recommendation letter or resources—but don't carry their burden home with you. You can only do so much. Operate with integrity, stay grounded, and let go of what you can't control.

Make it Plain

Here's another kind of conflict that shows up in almost every workplace (but I shouldn't even have to say it): misunderstandings that could've been cleared up with a simple conversation.

When I was stationed in Montgomery, Alabama—away from home but close enough to Atlanta to visit family every weekend—I often turned down my coworkers' invites. Lunches, after-work drinks, weekend outings—I always said no. Not because I didn't like them, but because I didn't drink, I valued my personal time, and I was grinding to finish my first book.

But instead of asking me why, they judged me and assumed I wasn't a team player. Before long, the invites stopped altogether, the conversations turned surface-level, and the vibe turned cold. Eventually, they even brought it up to a superior, and suddenly I was painted as the problem—even though I was performing well at my job.

One thing I know is that conflict that stems from assumptions festers in silence. And instead of addressing it openly, teams often single out one person, which only makes the situation worse. In my case, all it would've taken was an informal team huddle to clear the air. No drama, no judgment—just a little clarity.

So when misunderstandings creep in, don't let them grow legs. Call the team together, lay it out plain, and deal with it directly. Nine times out of ten, what feels like a big conflict is really just a lack of communication.

Flip the Mindset

First thing's first—when conflict pops up, don't panic and don't shut down. Train yourself to reframe it. Instead of seeing conflict as chaos, see it as clarity. Ask yourself: *How can this moment make my team better? How can this actually pull us closer instead of pushing us apart?*

Conflict is temporary. It passes. But the lessons you pull from it last.

Step into the Other Person's Shoes

We all process conflict through our own emotions, history, and triggers. Some people just can't "shake it off" and function like nothing happened. That's why handling conflict requires maturity. Sometimes, you've got to step back and ask: *If I were them, how would I feel right now?*

It's what I call "peeling back the onion." Don't just react to what's on the surface—dig for the root. Is this really about work, or is it personal? Is it a misunderstanding? The more you can see through their lens, the better chance you have of connecting and creating real resolution.

Focus on Learning, Not Winning

Too many people approach conflict like it's a battle to win. They're locked into proving a point instead of fixing the problem. But when you shift from "winning" to "learning," everything changes.

Ask: *What lesson can I take from this? How can I show up better as a leader because of it?* When you condition yourself to see conflict as a classroom, not a boxing ring, the whole team grows stronger.

Communication Should Be a Bridge, Not a Wall

Most leaders trip up when it comes to communication. Real talk: in conflict, the louder you yell, the less people hear. Communication isn't about dominating. It's about staying calm, being clear, and listening just as much as you speak.

And yes, sometimes you'll lead with clarity and integrity and people still won't want to hear it. Don't carry that home with you. Don't internalize it. People replay situations in their head all the time and realize later, *"It wasn't you, it was me."* Stay consistent. Keep showing up as the leader. Your integrity will always outlast any moment of resistance.

Know When to Pivot

Let me share a story my friend told me—she's a director for a theater troupe. She cast an actress in the lead role, but in rehearsal, this actress kept holding back. The team struggled to connect with her energy, and it was dragging everyone down.

The director gave her feedback, brought in mentors, had one-on-one talks—and still, nothing changed. Finally, the actress said, *"When the lights come up on opening night, I'll give you 100%."*

That sounds good, but leaders know people perform how

they practice. My friend couldn't risk her entire production on a "maybe." So, she pivoted—moved the actress to understudy and handed the lead role to someone else who was ready.

That's leadership. You communicate, you listen, you extend grace—but at some point, you draw the line. If someone won't rise to the occasion, you must protect your team, your brand, and your mission. Don't be afraid to pivot.

Stay Calm and Breathe

Your words matter. Once they're out, you can't snatch them back. That's why staying calm is non-negotiable. Share your thoughts, yes—but make sure you're also listening. Active listening shows respect for the other person's feelings, and once you've really digested what they've said, you can respond with clarity instead of heat.

Conflict has a way of pushing us into defense mode. Snapping back, getting loud, or shutting down might feel natural, but it only makes things worse. Instead, breathe. Speak with intent. Offer explanations without losing your cool. People respect a leader who can provide clarity without creating drama.

Active Listening

Most of us don't listen to understand—we listen to reply. That's not active listening.

To really listen means you're fully engaged. When someone steps into my office, I push my computer aside, silence my phone, and give them eye contact. I might nod, repeat back something they said, or ask a clarifying question just to show them I'm with them. That kind of presence builds trust and reduces conflict before it even has a chance to grow legs.

Keep Your Tone in Check

Sometimes it's not *what* you say—it's *how* you say it. Tone is everything. Defensive, condescending, or competitive tones shut people down fast. Respectful, steady, and clear tones open the door to real conversation.

Think of tone as your leadership instrument—use it wisely. If you lose control, people will either mirror your energy or retreat completely. Neither outcome solves the conflict.

Get to the Root of the Issue

Empathy is the secret weapon. It's not about being soft; it's about being real enough to say, *"I see you, I hear you, I respect you."* Once people feel that, the walls come down.

I once worked with a woman in the military who was constantly late. On the surface, it looked like a professionalism issue. Supervisors wrote her up. But when I finally sat down with her, she broke down—she was a newly divorced single mom trying to manage two kids on her own. Once she opened up, we were able to adjust her schedule so she could make up her time. Problem solved—not through punishment, but through empathy.

Another similar example is when a teacher friend of mine had a student who was always late to class. Naturally, she was frustrated. But when she pulled him aside, he revealed that he and his family were homeless, living in a car, and washing up at a gas station before school. That shifted everything. She bent the rules, letting him slip quietly through the back door so he wouldn't keep racking up tardy slips and face suspension for something he couldn't control.

What's the lesson here? Sometimes conflict isn't about rebellion or defiance   it's about circumstances. If you don't take the time to get to the root, you'll end up punishing people for things they have no power over. But when you dig deeper, you create space for compassion, understanding, and real solutions.

TOOLS FOR SUCCESS

Don't Just Solve the Problem—Address the Emotions

Too many leaders jump straight into "fix-it mode." Slow down. Before you can fix anything, you need to tune into how people *feel*. Sometimes the conflict isn't even about the actual problem—it's about the frustration, the fear, or the insecurity underneath it. Ask yourself: *What's really going on here emotionally?* When you get to the *why* behind the issue, solutions come easier.

Empathy Builds Bridges

At the end of the day, people are not machines—they're human beings with bills, families, struggles, and stress. If you can see past the "employee" label and treat them like a whole person, you shift the entire energy of the conversation. That's where trust and loyalty are born. People work harder and show up better when they know their leader actually cares.

Show Vulnerability

Real leaders don't have all the answers. And guess what? That's okay. Admitting when you don't know it all and inviting your team to figure it out with you is powerful. It shows strength, not weakness. Vulnerability gives your team permission to be honest too. That's how you build an environment where people feel safe to be real.

Pause and Process

When conflict pops off, don't just react—pause. Take a breath. Step back and give yourself a second to think. Ask: *What's really happening here? How can I respond instead of react?* That small pause is the difference between fanning the flames and calming the fire.

The Conflict Reflection Journal

After a conflict, write it out. Jot down what happened, how it made you feel, what you learned, and how you responded. Over time, you'll start to see patterns in the way you handle conflict. That journal becomes your playbook for growth—a way to track not just the drama but the lessons that come with it.

5 Questions to Ask Yourself in Any Conflict

1. **What's really going on here?**
   Am I reacting to the surface issue, or is there something deeper?

2. **How are they feeling right now?**
   Not just what they're saying—what emotions are driving their words?

3. **How am *I* feeling right now?**
   Am I calm enough to lead, or do I need a pause before I respond?

4. **What lesson is here for me?**
   Instead of focusing on "winning," what can I learn to lead better next time?

5. **What outcome do I want to create?**
   Do I want resolution, connection, clarity—or am I just trying to prove a point?

Conflict is part of the game. You can't dodge it, ignore it, or wish it away. But the good news is that it doesn't have to be destructive. When you step into conflict with self-awareness, empathy, and clarity, you turn it from drama into growth.

Being a leader isn't about "fixing" people or proving you're right—it's about creating a space where people feel heard, respected, and valued. That's how trust is built. That's how your team learns to lean in instead of check out.

And don't forget—your tone, your presence, your ability to stay grounded sets the temperature for the whole room. If you keep it calm, keep it clear, and keep it human, your team will mirror that energy. They'll see you don't just talk leadership—you live it.

At the end of the day, handling conflict with intention and heart is what separates mediocre leaders from the ones people would actually *ride for*. Because when you model real communication, empathy, and resilience, you're not just guiding a team through tough times—you're showing them how to come out stronger, tighter, and more connected on the other side.

That's leadership with authenticity. That's leadership with impact. That's leadership that lasts.

REFLECTIONS

_____

_____

_____

_____

_____

_____

_____

_____

_____

_____

_____

_____

_____

_____

_____

_____

_____

_____

_____

_____

_____

_____

_____

_____

_____

_____

_____

_____

_____

_____

_____

_____

_____

_____

_____

_____

_____

_____

_____

_____

_____

_____

_____

_____

_____

_____

_____

_____

_____

_____

_____

_____

_____

_____

_____

"RESPECT STARTS WHERE
OVEREXTENSION ENDS."

CHAPTER 6
DON'T LOSE YOURSELF

Leadership without boundaries is a fast track to burnout. Setting boundaries isn't about being cold, rigid, or standoffish—it's about protecting your energy, your values, and your team's trust. Think of boundaries as guardrails, not walls. They don't block people out; they show people the right way to come in.

I've seen far too many people—especially leaders—run themselves ragged because they don't know how to say no. They're stretched thin, overworked, and overwhelmed, yet they still answer every request, fix every problem, and carry everybody else's load while ignoring their own. And you know what that does? It leaves them tired, resentful, and with nothing left to give.

Parents are especially guilty of this. They'll give, give, and give some more because they love their kids, but they never take time to fill their own cup. Good intentions don't cancel out the damage. A lack of boundaries will drain you physically, mentally, and emotionally until you've got nothing left.

That's why boundaries matter. They protect more than just your time—they protect your peace, your focus, and your ability to show up strong for others.

I had to learn this lesson the hard way, even with people I love the most. Take my mom, for example. She's a traveler and would call me randomly in the middle of the day just to chat. And because she's my mom, I always picked up—even if I was knee-deep in writing or at work. But over time, I realized it was pulling me away from the focus I needed. I wasn't upset with her; I was upset with myself for not setting a boundary. So, I asked her to send a quick text before calling to make sure I was available. That small shift changed everything. She didn't feel neglected, and I didn't feel frustrated or distracted. That's the power of boundaries.

How did I use this in the workplace? Whew, that was a whole different story. I was known for being the first to arrive, the last to leave, and the go-to girl for fixing everybody's problems. On paper, that sounds good. In reality, I was exhausted. I barely ate lunch, skipped workouts, and carried the office home with me every night. I was the hero without a cape—and it almost broke me.

The turning point came when I finally started saying no. A polite but firm no became my full sentence. I refused to let people eat up my lunch hour, and I learned to delegate instead of carrying everyone's weight. That shift wasn't easy, but it saved my sanity. And guess what? People respected me more for it.

At the end of the day, boundaries don't make you less of a leader—they make you a better one. They keep you sharp, focused, and balanced, so you can lead with both compassion and clarity.

Unwavering Boundaries

Be clear on your nonnegotiables—the things you absolutely cannot compromise on. This could be family, health, faith, or specific leadership principles. Write it down. Put it on paper if you have to. No shame in that—it keeps you accountable and makes it crystal clear to yourself (and everybody else) what lines you won't let people cross. When you know what really matters, you give others a blueprint for how to value your time and respect your space.

A friend of mine told me about a woman director who worked on a film project. Now, if you know anything about film sets, you know they can run 14 hours a day easy—sometimes longer. Most directors would keep the cast and crew grinding late into the night just to "get the shot." But not this woman.

One evening, it was around 8 PM and the team had been running a scene over and over. She suddenly announced, *"That's a wrap!"* The crew looked around, confused. Somebody said, "But you didn't get the shot you wanted." And she said, "True. But I told y'all—8 o'clock, I'm done. I'm going home to put my kids to bed."

That's a nonnegotiable in action. She was willing to sacrifice the shot, but she wasn't about to sacrifice her values. And guess what? People respected her for it. Her boundary wasn't just a preference—it was a principle. And when leaders live by their principles, they teach everybody else around them that boundaries aren't weakness. They're strength.

Boundaries and Empathy Can Coexist

Before you start laying down a new boundary, slow down and *listen*. Don't just jump in with "this is how it is." Hear people out. When you show that you care, your boundary-setting won't feel like you're shutting people down—it feels like you're creating mutual respect. Explain why it matters, how it protects not only you but the team, and people are much more likely to accept it.

Communicate your boundaries upfront. Be clear about what's off limits, what you're prioritizing, and why. It's not about being selfish—it's about valuing yourself enough to protect your peace. And when you stand firm on your own boundaries, you'll often inspire others to finally set theirs too.

Now, I must warn you. Setting boundaries takes courage—especially if you've been operating without them for a while.

It might feel uncomfortable at first, and people may be surprised when you switch things up. But growth means moving differently once you know better. Don't be afraid to communicate your new boundaries. People who love you, respect you, or simply want to keep working with you will adjust.

A lot of us get stuck worrying about what people will think: *"But I've always done it this way. What will they say if I change it now?"* Let me stop you right there—it doesn't matter. If you discover something no longer works for you, you have every right to change it. Think about it: if strawberries always made your stomach hurt and the doctor finally told you you're allergic, would you keep eating them just because everyone else enjoys them? Absolutely not. You'd cut them out, no apologies. Boundaries work the same way—protect yourself from what you know isn't good for you, even if other people don't get it.

Stick to your word! If you let people cross your boundaries once, they'll keep testing you. Consistency is everything. Some people may not like the new rules. They might even claim that you're "acting brand new" or resent that you're no longer as available. But that's their issue, not yours. Protecting your mental health, productivity, and peace is worth the adjustment.

When you set a boundary, be firm but empathetic. Don't just drop a "take it or leave it" and walk off—explain the why, use a tone that shows you care, and leave space for further conversation. That way, people see you're not being harsh, you're just being intentional.

Most importantly, don't ever apologize for advocating for yourself. Boundaries aren't selfish—they're self-respect in action. I've gained so much confidence by creating strong boundaries, and I'm unapologetically vocal about them. You have that same right. So let me say it plain: the time is always now. Stop waiting, stop hesitating. Set your boundaries, stand on them, and protect your peace like your life depends on it—because in many ways, it does.

Respectful Reset

If someone crosses you, operates outside of integrity, or just flat-out disrespects you, don't sweep it under the rug. Address it right then and there—with respect. Passive-aggressive vibes help no one. Don't sit there knee-deep in your feelings pretending everything's fine. Speak up, clear the air, and then let it go.

Here's the formula I live by when someone steps out of line:

1. **Tell them what they did wrong.** Some people honestly don't even realize they've overstepped.

2. **Explain why it can't happen again.** Lay it out plain so they understand what's at stake.

3. **Tell them what you need from them moving forward.** Don't leave it up in the air.

4. **Explain why it matters.** Help them see the bigger picture—it's about respect, trust, and protecting the team.

This approach isn't aggressive; it's firm. And firm is necessary. It reinforces your boundaries, protects your energy, and shows people that while you may hold space for them, they still have to respect you.

Take undermining, for example. If somebody calls you out in front of the whole team, don't clap back right there and create a scene. Pull them aside and address it one-on-one. That way you keep it professional, but you still stand your ground. What you don't do is play games—ignoring them, stalling them, or finding sneaky ways to get "payback." Boundaries are about clarity, not pettiness.

Grace and Professionalism

Let me share a story. One of my actor friends had just taken on a role in a touring stage play. A new castmate straight-up mocked her during rehearsal—reading her lines out loud, stomping her feet, and acting like she knew better. To make it worse, other cast members laughed and clapped like they were at a comedy show. My friend could've snapped back, but she didn't. She let it play out.

Later that night, another actor chimed in with something constructive. She said the cast hadn't had time to build chemistry with her yet. My friend leaned into *that* truth instead of clapping back at the rude actress. She acknowledged the wisdom, thanked the actor for their honesty, and kept it moving.

Guess what? By the end of the first show, that same rude actress came up and said, "Your performance was so dope. You did well." That's growth. Sometimes people just need to see for themselves. And as leaders, we must give grace in the moment and let time be the teacher.

Praise the Good, Don't Just Police the Bad

Boundaries don't always mean calling people out. Sometimes the most powerful move is spotlighting positive behavior. Instead of dragging the one who's out of line, praise the one who's showing up right. A simple, "Susie, I love how focused you are right now. You're knocking it out!" shifts the energy of the whole room. People hear it, and they adjust without you ever having to raise your voice.

Boundaries Build Harmony

Boundaries of all kinds are necessary. They define your values, build mutual respect, and protect your peace. A lot of people avoid setting them because they're afraid of being misunderstood, called "difficult," or labeled a "diva." Sometimes the most loving thing you can do for your team and yourself is to be clear about what you need to perform at your best.

Boundaries aren't walls—they're bridges. They create order, protect energy, and make space for everyone to thrive. So don't back down. Stand firm, communicate clearly, and refuse to let anyone make you feel guilty for protecting your peace. That's leadership with heart, and that's how you create a team environment that actually works.

TOOLS FOR SUCCESS

Boundaries Build Respect, Not Resentment

You must understand that boundaries don't push people away, they show people how to treat you. When you hold firm on your limits, you're giving your team permission to do the same. You model what it looks like to take care of yourself without guilt. If your crew sees you saying, "Hey, I need to log off at 6," they'll feel safer doing the same—and guess what? Everybody wins because you're protecting peace, not creating tension.

One of my friends said it best: *"Boundaries don't shut people out—they show them how to enter."* When you stand on your values and keep it authentic, you become proof that it's possible to lead with strength *and* self-respect. Trust me, someone's watching how you move, and you're giving them courage to set their own boundaries too.

Reframe "No" as a Positive

Saying no isn't negative—it's actually saying yes to something else that matters. Think of it this way: saying no to a late-night meeting is saying yes to family dinner, or yes to your own rest so you can show up sharp tomorrow. Flip the script! Instead of beating yourself up, remind yourself that "no" is just a reroute to what's most important.

Address Pushback Head-On

I won't lie—when you start enforcing boundaries, some people will get salty. That's because they benefited from the old you, the "yes to everything" you. Don't fold. Stay calm, explain why the boundary matters, and keep it moving. And please note that you don't owe explanations to everybody, only to the people who are directly affected. Stop over-explaining yourself to the sidelines.

I've worked under leaders who didn't respect anybody's limits—they'd fire off emails at 2 AM or pile on tasks like we didn't have families waiting at home. That's not leadership— that's the epitome of being self-absorbed. Don't be that person. Respect other people's boundaries just like you want yours respected.

Have the Hard Conversations

Boundaries don't always feel warm and fuzzy. Sometimes they sting. But if your intentions are good, you've got to trust yourself and move forward. Deliver your truth with empathy, and then let people sit with their emotions. Not every situation can be explained away, and not everyone's gonna clap for your decisions—but boundaries aren't about pleasing, they're about preserving.

Do a Boundary Audit

Here's your assignment: grab 15 minutes and ask yourself—*Where am I drained? Where am I giving more than I'm getting back? Where am I saying "yes" out of guilt instead of alignment?* Write it down. That list is your blueprint.

Start small if you need to. Maybe this week, it's no more skipping lunch for other people's "urgent" requests. Next week, it's not answering late-night calls that throw you off your game. Step by step, you tighten the boundaries and protect your peace.

Because at the end of the day, boundaries aren't just for you—they make you a stronger, healthier leader for your team too.

Boundaries are not about being cold, difficult, or selfish. They're about respect—respect for yourself, your time, your values, and your team. When you set clear limits, you're not pushing people away—you're showing them how to treat you. And when you honor your own boundaries, you teach your team that it's okay for them to honor theirs, too.

I know it's not always easy. Especially if you've been the "yes" person for years, or if people are used to you always stretching yourself thin. At first, they may not like the new version of you that says *no* or that draws the line—but give it time. People who really value you will adjust, and those who don't…well, that tells you something right there.

Remember: your nonnegotiables are yours. Protecting your health, your peace, your family time, or simply your lunch break is not too much to ask. And if someone calls you "difficult" or "different" for finally putting yourself first, wear it like a badge of honor. That's growth.

As a leader, setting boundaries doesn't weaken your influence—it strengthens it. It shows you know how to manage yourself, your energy, and your team. It shows that you can balance compassion with clarity. And trust me, when your team sees you protecting your peace, they'll be more inspired to protect their own, which creates a healthier, more productive environment for everyone.

So don't be afraid to set the tone. Say no when you need to. Hold firm when it matters most. Communicate with grace, but stand on your word. Boundaries aren't walls—they're bridges that keep relationships strong and environments thriving.

Protect your peace, protect your energy, and watch how much better you show up—not just as a leader, but as a whole person.

REFLECTIONS

_____

_____

_____

_____

_____

_____

_____

_____

_____

_____

_____

_____

_____

_____

_____

_____

_____

_____

_____

_____

"NO IS A COMPLETE SENTENCE."

– ANNE LAMOTT

CHAPTER 7
MANAGING THE MESSY

Leadership isn't always pretty. Sometimes it's frustrating and downright exhausting. You'll have people on your team who test your patience, push your buttons, and make you question why you even signed up for this role in the first place. But the real measure of leadership isn't how you show up when everything's peaceful. Anybody can look good in calm waters. The test comes when the storm hits—when energy is off, personalities are clashing, and the room feels heavy. That's when you find out what kind of leader you really are.

True leadership is about holding your ground without losing your character, your compassion, or your confidence. It's about standing firm in who you are, while still creating space for other people to be seen, heard, and respected—even when they make it hard.

On a spiritual level, I believe people show up in our lives as mirrors. They reflect back the parts of ourselves that need attention, healing, or growth. That coworker with the bad attitude? That disrespectful client? That teammate who always seems to challenge you? They're not just a disruption to your day—they're a lesson in disguise.

When I face someone who rubs me the wrong way, I ask myself: *What are they here to teach me? What part of myself is being triggered right now? What lesson am I supposed to walk away with from this interaction?* Shifting the question changes the whole energy.

I am aware that none of it is random. God is intentional. Every challenge, every conflict, every "messy" moment is part of a bigger plan to sharpen you, grow you, and prepare you for what's next. Whether the situation feels good or bad, it's shaping you into a stronger, wiser, more grounded leader.

Challenging People Aren't the Problem— How You Handle Them Is

Look, not everybody is going to be easy to lead. Some people come with attitude, resistance, or straight-up drama. And while it's easy to slap the "difficult" label on them, people act out for a reason. Hurt, insecurity, fear, ego—it all shows up in different ways. The real challenge isn't just about *them*— it's about *you.* How do you show up when somebody's testing your patience? Do you clap back, get defensive, or shut down? Or do you stay grounded, listen, and respond with strategy instead of emotion?

Life has taught me that some of my hardest interactions weren't accidents—they were training. Looking back, I can see that if I hadn't gone through certain situations, I wouldn't have been equipped for what came later. That's why, these days, when I cross paths with someone "difficult," I try not to make it personal. Instead, I ask: *What am I supposed to gain from this? How can I grow from this moment? What part of me is being sharpened right now?*

Let me give you a simple example. Say your personal life is out of order—your house is a mess, your car looks like a storage unit, and you're running late to everything. Then, at work, there's Claire. Claire's desk is a disaster: folders everywhere, crumbs on the keyboard, chaos on full display. And every time you walk past, you're annoyed. But if you care to know the truth—Claire is just mirroring back to you the disorder you've been ignoring in your own life. Instead of pointing fingers, the real growth comes when you pause and say, *Okay, what about her chaos is triggering me? And how can I clean up my own?*

It's the same when you're putting yourself out there. Say you host an event, and people you love don't show up to support. That stings, right? But maybe that moment isn't about them at all—it's about you finally learning how to show up for *yourself*. Sometimes your outer world can't reflect what your inner world isn't ready to receive. You want love, but you won't love yourself. You want opportunities, but you won't prepare. The question becomes: *Do you enjoy your own company? Do you know what it feels like to laugh by yourself, to date yourself, to sit in quiet and still feel full?* If the answer is no, how can you expect someone else to show up for you in ways you won't show up for yourself?

And yes, all of this applies at work too. In earlier chapters, we talked about being the example you want others to follow. If you're late, but you expect your team to be on time, guess what? They're going to mirror your lateness. If you show up disorganized or negative, your team will reflect that energy back to you. People are mirrors—plain and simple.

Now, let's talk projection. Ever met someone quiet and automatically assumed, "They don't like me"? That's projection. They might just be introverted, shy, or anxious. But when we project our own fear of rejection onto them, we block the chance for a genuine connection. On the flip side, maybe you run into someone loud and obnoxious. My natural instinct isn't to be loud, but I give grace because I know what it exposes in me—the younger me who didn't use her voice, the part of me that sometimes still plays small, the part that can be intimidated. That "loud" person is showing me what needs strengthening inside myself.

Even things that shock or offend us—like someone being sexually liberated and talking openly about it—can be mirrors. If it stirs discomfort, it might be exposing suppressed parts of ourselves, things we haven't addressed or fully accepted.

Again, it's not always about them. It's about what gets stirred up in *you*.

Now, this doesn't mean we excuse unethical behavior. If someone's stealing, lying, or crossing moral lines, that's a different story. I'm strictly talking about personality clashes and character quirks here.

At the end of the day, managing messy people is about self-reflection and grace. Ask yourself: *What part of me is this exposing? How can I approach this with maturity, empathy, and strategy?* When you start viewing people as trainers instead of tormentors, you realize they're just here to build your muscle. That annoying coworker? They're teaching you patience. That boss with the constant early-morning emails? They're teaching you discipline. Those challenges are shaping you, not breaking you.

Don't Take the Bait

When somebody's trying to push your buttons, don't give them the satisfaction of seeing you snap. Some people thrive off chaos—if they know they can throw you off with drama, they'll keep doing it. Your power move is to stay calm, professional, and steady. Don't match their energy, don't feed the fire. Control your emotions, control the room. That's not weakness—that's strategy. Handle them with facts, not feelings, and you'll always come out ahead.

To tell the truth, some people will just want to get under your skin. (Blame poor parenting if you must.) But sometimes the messy *is* intentional. People see you as polished, put together, "having it all," and they'll poke just to prove you don't. They want to rattle you, make you look messy, and chip away at the respect you've earned. That's why it's so important not to take the bait. Don't let their bad day become yours.

Other times, though, it's not that deep. It's not even personal—it's just a miscommunication or misunderstanding. But if you live in your feelings, you'll treat every little thing like an attack, and that'll drain you quick. You have to train your internal dialogue to say, *this isn't about me.* Whether the button-pushing is intentional or not, your job is the same. And that's to stay as cool as a cucumber and unbothered.

People may test boundaries to see how far they can go but respect is non-negotiable. Even if you're not everybody's favorite, they still need to respect the position and the space you hold. It is important that you don't internalize every action. Sometimes people aren't trying to frustrate you—they're just moving how they move, by their own standards. That's why it's on you to filter it, address it professionally, and keep it moving.

When necessary, call it out: "Here's what's not okay, here's why it matters, and here's how we need to move forward." That way, you make it plain without losing your cool.

See the Human, Not Just the Behavior

I've learned to look past the bad attitude and see the *person.* Because most times, someone's reaction to you is coming from a deeper place: pain, fear, stress, or something they haven't healed yet. That doesn't mean you excuse the behavior or let it slide, but it does mean you lead with empathy instead of ego. When I separate *who they are* from *how they're acting,* I find myself leading with clarity instead of contempt. It's not about me—it's about understanding where they're really coming from.

Take my uncle, for example. At the time of writing this book, we'd only just found out he was dealing with a terminal illness. The smallest things could set him off—he would flip out over something minor, and my mom would get her feelings hurt. I had to remind her, "Don't take it personal." His behavior wasn't about her at all. He was battling something heavy, and his words were really displaced language for his pain. That doesn't mean the sting of his words didn't hurt—it did—but we had to recognize the bigger picture.

That's what leadership calls for sometimes: putting yourself in other people's shoes and remembering their humanity, even when their actions don't reflect it. They're still a mirror. They still reflect back something for you to learn—whether it's patience, compassion, or just the ability to pause before reacting.

The roles could always be reversed. Tomorrow, you could be the one under pressure, lashing out, or misunderstood. That's why when your heart is really for people—to see them well, do well, and grow—you'll find that extra ounce of compassion. That doesn't mean you let disrespect slide; it means you choose to handle the moment from a place of grace and leadership, not frustration.

Set Clear Expectations and Boundaries

People can't respect what you've never made clear. Period. If you don't lay out your expectations upfront, you leave room for misunderstandings, excuses, and a whole lot of unnecessary drama. But when you make things plain—"Here's what I expect, here's how we roll, and here's what happens if we don't"—you take the guesswork out of it. Everybody knows where the line is drawn.

Now, boundaries are not about controlling people. A lot of people get that twisted. Boundaries are about creating *clarity*. And clarity is what keeps the team flowing without confusion or resentment. When you've communicated openly and set the standard, you don't have to argue later about what's fair. There's no, "Well, I didn't know" or "You didn't say that." No, it's already been said, and it's already been agreed to.

That's what makes consequences easier to enforce. Because it's not personal—it's procedural. You're not coming out of nowhere with some random punishment; you're simply following through on what you already made clear from the start. That consistency not only protects your authority but also builds trust. People may not always *like* your boundaries, but they'll respect them because they know you're fair and you mean what you say.

Keep Your Receipts

I'll be real—feelings don't hold up when conflict pops off. Facts do. That's why you've got to keep your receipts. Don't rely on memory alone when people cross lines or ignore boundaries. Document everything—emails, texts, group chats, call logs—whatever you can get your hands on. That way, if things ever turn into a "he said, she said," you've got proof, not just vibes.

And if someone comes at you sideways verbally, shut it down right there and move it to paper. Don't waste your peace arguing back and forth. Simply say, "Let's continue this over email," and document the exchange. Now you're not stuck trying to convince anyone with your word alone—you've got the receipts to back it up.

Sometimes, though, receipts aren't enough. That's when you call in reinforcement. My homegirl works as a security officer, and I was on the phone with her one day while she was at work. I could hear her checking people in, being her usual professional self. Then someone came up to her and asked her to remove a lady from a room she wasn't supposed to be in. She told my friend, "I just need you to be here with me so she can't say I said something I didn't." Boom—that's protocol. She brought backup so nobody could twist the story later.

Same thing happened to me once when I was a First Sergeant. One of my troops started following me on Facebook. At first, no big deal—until he slid into my DMs making inappropriate comments on my workout photos. (Mind you, these were normal, professional pictures.) That was a hard line crossed. When it came time to address it, I didn't go in alone. I brought a third party into the meeting with me. Why? Because I wasn't about to risk my career on his version of the story. With another witness in the room, it was clear, professional, and documented.

Bottom line: cover yourself. Protect your peace with facts, not feelings. Write it down. Save the receipts. Bring backup if you need to. You don't owe anyone drama, but you *do* owe yourself the protection of your reputation, your career, and your peace of mind.

Grace Is Not Weakness—It's Strategy

In case you thought otherwise, giving grace doesn't mean letting people walk all over you. Grace isn't about tolerating chaos or disrespect. Grace is about giving people room to grow while keeping your standards intact. When you lead with grace, you shift the power dynamic. You're not on defense, clapping back or lashing out—you're on offense, moving with wisdom. That's strength.

I'll give you an example. I once worked with someone who just wasn't herself anymore. Reports were late, she skipped team meetings, and when she did show up, her attitude was sharp. I wasn't even her first-line leader, but I knew something was off, so I pulled her aside and we went for a walk. Within minutes, she broke down. Her dad was sick in the hospital, her husband was having an affair, and she was running on fumes. No sleep, no peace at home—just trying to hold it together.

Now, I didn't excuse her missed deadlines or her attitude. But I did extend grace by creating a safe space for her to talk. I told her: "If you want me to protect you, you have to help me by showing up professionally." That's grace—meeting people where they are, but still reminding them of the standard.

But let's also talk about "fake grace." You know what I mean—that passive-aggressive front people put on and call it grace. I worked with a woman once who had a major issue with her team lead. She never spoke to him directly, but she sure spoke to everyone else. She'd walk around loudly quoting scripture—"Vengeance is mine, saith the Lord!" and "God's gonna work this out for me!"—but never once addressed the conflict. That wasn't grace. That was bitterness dressed up in holy language.

And it backfired. At the end of the project, the team lead—

who still had the power—left her out of the awards ceremony. Everyone got recognized except her. In front of a room full of people, she was embarrassed. When you meet negativity with negativity, everybody loses. Quoting scripture won't cover up spiteful behavior. Grace isn't about looking holy—it's about being whole.

Real grace says: *"Yes, you hurt me, but I forgive you. I won't return your energy. I choose peace."* It doesn't mean you ignore the issue. It doesn't mean there are no consequences. It means you rise above the urge to get even, because grace keeps you free.

Protect the Culture, Not Just Your Ego

Leadership can't be about your ego. If you're in it to prove a point, you've already lost. Leadership is about the environment you create for the people you're leading. It's about protecting the culture you're building—not feeding your pride.

So, check the drama at the door and deal with conflict head-on. Hold people accountable. Don't sweep issues under the rug, and definitely don't let one bad attitude poison the whole team. The minute you allow negativity to run wild, you're setting yourself up for higher turnover, low morale, and people who are just showing up for a paycheck instead of showing up with purpose.

Your job as a leader isn't to win arguments—it's to protect the vibe, the vision, and the values of the team. When you keep that front and center, the whole squad benefits.

Use Direct, Clear Language

Honestly, too many people dance around the truth when it needs to be said. Don't sugarcoat it. Don't water it down. Say exactly what you mean, mean what you say, and leave no room for confusion. You can be clear without being cruel, but clarity has to come first.

People who sugarcoat usually do it out of fear. Fear of

being judged. Fear of somebody not liking them. Fear of losing their shot. And that fear shows up everywhere—not just at work. It creeps into relationships too. Instead of saying, "Hey, I really hate when you leave your shoes in the middle of the floor," somebody will huff, stomp, or silently stew because they're scared of how the other person will respond.

The problem is that dancing around the issue only creates more tension. You're not helping yourself, and you're not helping the other person. So stop talking in circles and start standing in your truth.

Now, does this mean you need to bark orders or cut people down? Absolutely not. It's not *what* you say—it's *how* you say it. Speak with professionalism and respect, but be direct. If someone challenges you for being honest, that's on them. Their reaction is their responsibility.

At the end of the day, leadership isn't about being liked—it's about being clear, being fair, and keeping it real. Fear clouds the message. Truth sets it straight.

Sometimes You Gotta Have the Hard Conversation

As much as some believe this, avoiding conflict doesn't keep the peace. All it does is buy time until the whole thing blows up. As a leader, your job isn't just to manage projects and check boxes—it's to have the conversations nobody else wants to have. Please know that challenging personalities don't get better with silence. They get bolder.

I saw this play out with a coworker who avoided a tough conversation she desperately needed to have. Instead of addressing the root issue, she let little things pile up. What started as one problem turned into many, and eventually two leaders ended up screaming at each other in front of the team. We had to send them both home for the day. Why? Because one person didn't use her voice when it mattered. She admitted later that she avoids conflict because her parents never dealt with issues growing up. When you're in leadership, you don't get to choose silence. Silence breeds chaos.

You have to train yourself to use your voice, even with the small stuff. Start at home if you have to. If your kids leave toothpaste in the sink, don't just sigh and clean it up. Call it out: *"Excuse me, this needs to be handled right now."* That small act builds the muscle for bigger conversations. You don't start running marathons without training; you build your endurance over time. Same thing with conflict.

Most people love hearing praise, but get all in their feelings when it's time for correction, even if it's constructive. That's fine. Your job isn't to keep everybody comfortable—it's to keep the team accountable. Grace and truth can coexist. You can be respectful *and* direct at the same time.

But if you know conflict shuts you down to the point where you freeze, don't ignore it. Get help. Counseling or coaching can literally help you role-play those hard conversations until you feel stronger having them in real life. Because pretending issues don't exist is the fastest way to wreck your team's trust, morale, and productivity.

At the end of the day, leadership requires courage. Use your voice. Speak your truth. Have the hard conversations before they snowball into something bigger.

TOOLS FOR SUCCESS

Stick to the Facts

Stay focused on the behaviors and not about how you felt attacked. While your feelings may be valid, stick to the facts to keep things tight. In other words, get out your feelings. Challenging personalities can trigger you and emotions can take over and cloud the conversation to the point that the facts and what you need to address gets lost in the shuffle. Keep it clean and classy.

Set the Tone

As a leader, you decide what atmosphere you want to create the moment you step into a room. If you walk in nervous, flustered, or angry, your team will mirror that energy right back at you. That's why it's your job to set the tone with calm confidence. Even when things get tense, your presence should say, *"I'm not here to argue; I'm here to lead, guide, and teach."*

And don't be fooled—successful leaders don't just wing it. They move with intention. That means having policies and practices in place and a game plan for the tough conversations. You don't need to read off a script, but you *do* need to know your talking points and the outcome you expect. If you're addressing an issue in a meeting, come prepared—with facts, references, and a clear direction. That way, no one can poke holes in what you're saying, and you stay in control.

Leading with intention builds trust. Your team learns that even when the energy is off, they can count on you to bring order, clarity, and focus back into the room.

The Energy Inventory or Audit

Once a week, I take about ten minutes to do what I call an *energy audit.* I sit with myself and think about the people I'm connected to—clients, colleagues, even family—and I ask three simple questions: *Who's draining me? Who's fueling me? Who could use my guidance?* This little check-in keeps me aware of how others impact me, but also how I might be impacting them. It helps me decide where I need stronger boundaries and where I need to lean in and show up differently.

But it's not just about other people. You've got to know your own *energetic baseline.* In other words, what does it feel like when you're at peace? What does it feel like when that peace is interrupted? If you can identify your "normal," you'll catch yourself quicker when things get off balance.

Life isn't about being on 10 all the time. The real goal is neutrality—not too high, not too low, just steady. That's why we're called *human beings*—not "human doings," not "human reactors." When you wake up in the morning, unless you dragged yesterday's drama into today, you start out neutral. From there, how you set the tone—what you think, say, or do first—determines if your day rises into joy or slides into gloom.

Don't be mistaken. Other people's energy will always show up. Maybe you woke up late, spilled coffee on yourself, and then that negative email came through. If your morning already started off rocky, that email is just going to magnify the funk. But when you know your baseline, you can catch yourself and pivot. You can say, *"Hold up, I'm not going to let this spiral."* You shift your focus, redirect your energy, and remind yourself that you're in control of how you show up.

Even as a leader, you're not immune to sudden shifts in energy—but you are responsible for managing yours. Awareness plus accountability is the secret. When you protect your energy, you protect your peace—and that safeguards not only you, but also your team and the position you hold.

Leadership isn't always pretty. Some days, it's uncomfortable and straight-up draining. But the real ones don't run from the hard stuff—we lead through it. Challenging personalities aren't a threat, they're an opportunity to lead with strategy, grace, and backbone. When you learn how to manage the messy without losing your mind or your integrity, you become the kind of leader people remember. Not because you were loud but because you were solid, steady, and respected.

Let them be messy. Stay grounded. Stay clear. And never forget—grace is power, and boundaries are love with structure. That's how a real one leads.

Managing the messy isn't for the faint of heart. People will test you, personalities will clash, and energy will get funky. Your job isn't to match chaos with more chaos. Your job is to lead with clarity, compassion, and control.

When people push your buttons, don't let them see you sweat. Handle it with facts, not feelings. When the vibe is off, set the tone yourself—calm, steady, and unshakable. And when you feel your peace slipping, do that energy inventory check. Ask yourself: *Am I operating from my best self, or am I letting somebody else's storm pull me under?*

"Messy" moments are just part of leadership, but they're also opportunities. Opportunities to grow, to teach, and to show your team what real strength looks like. Not loud, not reactive, not ego-driven—but steady, professional, and rooted in grace.

So, don't run from the messy. Step into it with wisdom and heart. Protect your energy, keep your receipts, and lead with a presence that says, *I got this.* Because when you manage the mess without losing yourself, your team learns that they can trust you to guide them through anything. That's leadership at its finest.

REFLECTIONS

"YOU GET WHAT YOU TOLERATE."

– HENRY CLOUD

CHAPTER 8
STAY HUNGRY

This final chapter is about staying hungry—not for titles, not for applause, but for growth. Real leaders don't peak— they evolve. The moment you get too comfortable is the moment you stop being effective. Leadership is not a finish line, it's a lifestyle. If you're not learning, stretching, and challenging yourself, then you're just managing. Honestly, managers maintain, but leaders multiply. So let's focus on what it takes to embrace growth with grit, humility, and what it means to have that unshakable drive to level up.

The rank, the title, the accolades—they're cool, but they don't keep you sharp. Growth does. Growth is what keeps you valuable and respected even when the uniform comes off. Real ones know: your role might change, but your responsibility to grow never ends. The second you think you've "arrived" is the second you start slipping.

A leader who's just managing is basically checking boxes. They're mission-driven but blind to the people doing the work. They miss the human factor. I remember working for AT&T, stuck in traffic because of a bad accident. Another teammate had a family emergency that same morning. Guess what? We were all written up. There was no grace. No empathy. Just punishment for not being on time. That's management, not leadership. They cared about rules, not people.

And that's the danger of leaders who always "go by the book." On paper, they look consistent. In reality, they're showing fear or insecurity—afraid to bend, afraid to think critically, afraid to stand on their own judgment. Protocol becomes their crutch. But real leadership is about discernment. Can you recognize when an exception should be made? Do you know when to risk stepping outside the script? A good leader has the confidence to go against the grain and stand firm on their decision—even when it's not popular. A friend of mine had a supervisor who knew she didn't deserve a write-up after being in a car accident that made her only ten minutes late. She had proof—time-stamped police report, called 30 minutes ahead, everything. But the supervisor still wrote her up because another manager said, "Well, last year I got written up in a similar situation, so it wouldn't be fair." Instead of standing on her authority, she folded.

That's what happens when you lead by fear of perception instead of confidence in your judgment. A stronger leader would've said, "No, this is different. She did everything right. She's not being penalized on my watch." Compassion backed by authority—that's what real leadership looks like.

Sometimes leadership requires you to say, "I know what the book says, but I'm the leader in this moment. My call stands." That's not weakness; that's wisdom. It's emotional intelligence. It's integrity. Yes, you risk someone whispering "favoritism," but when you know your decision is grounded in fairness and humanity, you can stand ten toes down. And the key is communication. If you can clearly explain why you made the call, most people will respect you for it—even if they don't agree.

Growth Is a Requirement, Not a Reward

The evidence of a leader's growth isn't just in their résumés—it shows up in their team. Think of it like this: imagine two second-grade classrooms that started the school year wild, rowdy, and behind in reading. One teacher learns new strategies, keeps the kids focused, and helps them raise their reading and math scores by 20%. The other spends the year still yelling over the noise, and her students only improve by 5%. Which teacher grew? Exactly—the first one. But notice, her growth didn't just show up in her—it showed up in her students. The same is true for leadership. The progress of your team—their focus, their results, their culture—will always reflect your own growth.

Another way to check your growth is by looking at how you handle conflict now versus how you used to. I'll be transparent—in the past, if I felt a younger leader was being disrespectful, my first instinct was to snap back. Now? I pull them aside, address it calmly, and make it clear that disrespect won't fly without losing my cool. That's growth—responding with authority and composure instead of emotion. And let's not forget the numbers. Growth isn't just a "feeling." Sometimes it's in the data. Whether it's quality assurance in a call center, attendance records, or performance scores, the numbers don't lie. They can show you whether you're improving or just standing still.

Sometimes growth doesn't look glamorous at all. It looks like admitting you're coasting and you've been on autopilot longer than you want to admit. Comfort can sneak up on you disguised as "stability," and before you know it, you're bored, irritated, and unmotivated, wondering what happened. That feeling is not failure; it's a signal. It's your life tapping you on the shoulder saying, "You've outgrown this version of yourself." Real growth means raising your own standard when nobody is asking you to and nobody is watching. It's deciding that "good enough" is not the place you plan to retire.

Growth also requires boundaries with yourself, not just

with other people. It's easy to call something "busy" when it's really avoidance. Some people hide from growth by staying overbooked so they don't have to face the conversation they've been dodging, the decision they won't make, or the habit they refuse to break. Look at your calendar—does it show purpose or just motion? Leaders don't just add more to their plate; they choose what actually matters and let the rest fall away. That takes courage because people will not always like your new no. But the version of you that's committed to growing will thank you later.

Another sign of real growth is how you handle being wrong. In the past, some of us would defend a bad decision just to protect our pride. Now, growth sounds like, "You're right—I missed it, and here's how I'm fixing it." People trust leaders who can own mistakes without spiraling into shame or blaming everybody else in the room. Your ego will want the last word, but your maturity will choose the right one. When your team sees you apologize and then get back to work, you give them permission to be human and accountable at the same time. That's how cultures shift—quietly, consistently, through example.

Long-term leadership is also about staying healthy enough to last. Burning yourself out and calling it dedication is a trap a lot of high achievers fall into. Rest is not laziness; it's maintenance for your mind, body, and judgment. Tired leaders make sloppy decisions and short-tempered comments that take weeks to repair. When you build rhythms that include rest, reflection, and honest check-ins with yourself, you don't just feel better—you lead better. Your team watches how you treat yourself and learns from that too. At some point the question becomes: are you just leading for today, or are you building a version of yourself who can lead well five and ten years from now?

TOOLS FOR SUCCESS

Weekly Reflections Are Key

Growth doesn't just fall in your lap—you've got to be intentional. Carve out time every week to check in with yourself. Reflection lets you celebrate the wins (big or small) and also forces you to be honest about where you missed the mark. Ask yourself: *Could I have handled that conflict better? Did I show up for my team the way I should have?* What you don't acknowledge, you repeat—so stop running in circles. Get in the habit of having a "meeting with yourself." Books, workshops, and conferences can spark the reflection process too, but it starts with you taking the time.

Ego-Killing Feedback

Compliments feel good, but they don't grow you. Growth comes from the truth that stings a little. You've got to be open to constructive criticism from people you trust—mentors, friends, coaches who won't sugarcoat it. It might bruise your ego, but it'll also build your muscle. Remember, comfort doesn't create growth. Discomfort does.

Better Circles

You don't always have to reinvent the wheel. Sometimes the smartest move is to learn from somebody who's already walked the road you're trying to take. That's where mentorship comes in. If you feel stagnant or you're always the sharpest person in the room, it's time to level up your circle. Find leaders with more wisdom, more experience, more success, and sit at their table. Drop the ego, study their journey, and soak up their lessons—wins and losses. Growth multiplies in the right company.

Get Uncomfortable on Purpose

Comfort zones are leadership killers. If you're not being stretched, you're getting stale. Your dreams should scare you a little. If they don't, you're playing too small. Push yourself daily—volunteer for that tough assignment, present in front of the big crowd, or finally tackle the thing you've been avoiding. Steel sharpens steel, not pillows. Growth hides in the very things you run from, so lean in.

Don't Let Your Title Outgrow Your Character

A title without character is just noise. Growth without integrity is dangerous. Real leadership isn't about your job description—it's about how you treat people when nobody's watching. Keep your word, stay humble, and check your motives: are you chasing influence or impact? Remember, your title can disappear overnight, but your reputation sticks for life. Never forget the golden rule—treat the janitor the same way you treat the CEO. That's the kind of growth that matters most.

Here are a few things you can do to stretch yourself:

- o   Take on a new responsibility that scares you a little.
- o   Ask someone to coach you in an area where you're weak.
- o   Volunteer to speak, present, or lead something outside your normal lane.
- o   Do the things you avoid—those are usually where the growth is hiding.
- o   Embrace failure as feedback—not defeat.

Don't Let Your Title Outgrow Your Character

Growth without character is dangerous. A title without integrity is just noise. You've got to grow inwardly just as much as you grow upwardly. Leadership maturity isn't about your job description—it's about how you treat people when nobody's watching. Keep your name clean, your word solid, and your mindset humble.

For example, I came across a video where little boys were waiting for an autograph after a tennis match. The athlete kindly handed the hat from his head over to one of the little boys, but an adult male standing next to him reached for the cap and quickly claimed it as his own. The little boy reached his hand out to receive it from the adult, but it was ignored. Later, the athlete found the boy and gifted him with autographed souvenirs for his misfortune. However, the people on social media wouldn't let it rest. They discovered that the hat-taker was the CEO of a long-standing company and set out to destroy him. I mean, come on! Who takes from kids?

He ultimately made a statement that went something like "finders keepers, losers weepers," which was a reflection of his character—whether onlookers like it or not. I don't advise that you do the same. His business may continue to thrive, but that moment will live rent free on the internet and in people's memories.

Here is what you can do to ensure your character is in check:

- o Self-check your motives—are you chasing influence or impact?
- o Stay accountable. Let someone call you out without ego.
- o Treat the janitor like the general.
- o Check your pride—your title can be gone tomorrow, but your reputation sticks.
- o Remember the golden rule: to treat others the way you would want to be treated.

Leaders who stop growing, stop leading—point blank. Period. The moment you think you've "arrived" is the moment you start slipping. Staying hungry isn't about chasing another stripe on your sleeve, another title on your resume, or another pat on the back. It's about staying humble enough to know you don't know it all, teachable enough to learn from anyone, and bold enough to keep stretching past your comfort zone.

Real leadership is a lifestyle—it's about building character that can't be bought, creating impact that outlives titles, and showing others what it looks like to keep evolving no matter the season you're in. If you stay hungry, your leadership will stay fresh, relevant, and magnetic.

So never stop feeding your growth. Read, reflect, take risks, ask questions, and let life stretch you. Because the day you stop learning is the day you stop leading. Stay sharp. Stay grounded. Stay hungry. Always.

REFLECTIONS

_____

_____

_____

_____

_____

_____

_____

_____

_____

_____

_____

_____

_____

_____

_____

_____

_____

_____

_____

_____

_____

_____

_____

_____

_____

_____

_____

_____

_____

_____

_____

_____

_____

_____

_____

_____

_____

_____

_____

"IF THEY'RE OFFENDED BY YOUR
LIMITS, THEY WERE BENEFITING FROM
YOUR LACK OF THEM."

CONCLUSION
PASS THE MIC

By now you should know that leadership isn't just about how loud your voice is when you're in the room. It's about what echoes when you leave. Legacy isn't built on résumés, plaques, or titles; it's built in the people you poured into, the doors you held open, and the cycles you helped break.

Real leaders don't hog the spotlight—they *share* it. They pass the mic, they pull up a chair, and they make space on purpose. That's mentorship. That's sponsorship. That's how you take the blessings you've been given and multiply them in somebody else's life.

What good is winning if you're the only one at the finish line? The real flex is reaching back, grabbing somebody else's hand, and saying, "Come on, let's go higher together." That's not just leadership—that's legacy.

You Don't Have to Hold the Mic to Have Power

A lot of us grew up fighting for the mic—fighting to be heard, seen, and respected. And don't get it twisted, that fight was real and it mattered. But real power isn't in clutching the mic 'til your knuckles turn white. Real power is knowing when to pass it.

When you hand somebody else that mic, you're not losing shine—you're multiplying light. You're saying, "I don't just lead for me, I lead so *we* can win." That's when leadership stops being about ego and starts being about impact. That's when the work you do turns into legacy.

Here is how to ensure you make an impact that outlives your presence:

Identify someone with potential who needs a platform. Leadership is about having an eye for potential, even when the person doesn't fully see it in themselves. Maybe it's that team member who always has great ideas but never speaks up in meetings, or the one who shows quiet consistency behind the scenes. True leaders don't just chase stars—they recognize seeds and invest in them. Look for the people who are ready for more but just need someone to believe in them and call it out.

Give them opportunities to lead, speak, or show up differently. It's one thing to tell someone they have potential—it's another to actually hand them the reins. Let them run the meeting, present the project, or represent the team at an event. That kind of exposure not only builds their confidence, but it also shows others that you trust them. And trust is contagious—once they feel it from you, they start walking taller and others begin to see them differently too.

Step back—but don't disappear. Be a guide, not a gatekeeper. Passing the mic doesn't mean abandoning the stage. Your role shifts from being the main voice to being the coach in the corner, offering feedback, encouragement, and guidance when needed. Don't hover or smother, but make it clear you're there if they stumble. The goal is to empower them to stand on their own while knowing they've still got a safety net.

Remember: Mentorship is private. Sponsorship is public. Do both. Mentorship happens behind the scenes—it's those real conversations, quiet corrections, and encouragement that help someone sharpen their skills. Sponsorship, on the other hand, is when you put your reputation on the line to publicly vouch for them, recommend them, or create doors they wouldn't otherwise walk through. Great leaders don't stop at mentorship— they go the extra mile and sponsor people into spaces where their names can be heard in rooms they're not even in. If you want your impact to echo, you've got to do both.

Legacy Is What People Say When You're Not in the Room

Legacy isn't built through big speeches or job titles—it's built through how you treat people, how you lead in the quiet moments, and how you show up consistently. If the only thing you're leaving behind is a title on a plaque, you missed it.

Lead in a way that teaches others how to lead. Don't just lead for the sake of getting things done—lead in a way that models what leadership should look like. The people watching you today will be the ones carrying the torch tomorrow, so your style, your decisions, and your character will echo in how they lead. Think about it: are you teaching them how to bark orders, or how to build trust? Every interaction is a classroom, whether you realize it or not. Set an example that you'd actually be proud to see multiplied.

Pour into people without making them feel like they owe you. Real mentorship isn't about keeping score. If every time you help someone, you remind them of it later, then you weren't pouring—you were investing for a return. The point of pouring into people is to help them grow, not to create a debt. When people know your support comes with no strings attached, they can receive it freely and, more importantly, they're more likely to pour into others too. That's how you start a ripple effect of generosity in leadership.

Build something that outlasts your name on the email list. Your influence can't just live in your inbox or on your title card. Think about the systems, the culture, or even the mindsets you're instilling that will still exist when you're no longer there. When people walk into that office, that classroom, or that organization, will they feel the foundation you laid? That's the kind of legacy that lives on—not your name in a file, but the environment you built and the values you embedded into it.

Ask yourself weekly: If I left tomorrow, what would still stand because of me? This is the gut-check question every leader needs to sit with. If you had to walk away today, what would remain? Would your team be stronger, more capable, and more confident because of your influence—or would everything fall apart without you there? Leadership that leaves a legacy is about building people up to stand on their own. If they can keep going without you, then you've done your job.

If You Open the Door, Leave It Unlocked

Legacy leadership isn't about raising up little "mini-me's." It's about widening the circle, making sure the next wave of leaders looks even more bold, diverse, and unstoppable than the last. Too often, people only pour into people who remind them of themselves—the ones who look like them, talk like them, or lead the way they do. But the world doesn't grow like that. Real leaders use their influence to bring new voices to the table and make sure people who've never had a mic in their hand get a chance to speak, shine, and show what they're made of.

Don't just mentor people who look, talk, or lead like you. If you're only pouring into people who mirror you, you're not really mentoring—you're just multiplying yourself. And that's lazy leadership. Growth happens when you stretch beyond your comfort zone. Find people who see the world differently than you, who grew up with different challenges, who think in ways that make you pause. That's how you grow, and that's how the whole team levels up.

Normalize diversity in leadership. Advocate for it. Diversity isn't a checkbox—it's a cheat code. Different voices at the table mean fresh ideas, new perspectives, and better solutions. But it doesn't just "happen." Leaders have to speak up for it, push for it, and create space for it. So don't just clap when someone mentions diversity—be the one in the room saying, "Nah, we need more women here. We need more color in this conversation. We need more perspectives at this table." That's how you shift culture.

When you learn the game, share the playbook. There's no honor in hoarding what you know. Somebody once helped you, whether you admit it or not. So when you crack the code—when you figure out how to move in a room full of power, how to negotiate a contract, or how to navigate the politics—don't keep it to yourself. Pass the game along. Imagine how much further you would've been if somebody gave you the real from the jump. Be that person. Sharing your wisdom doesn't take away your shine; it makes sure the light spreads.

Don't just leave the door open—go back and bring people through. Leaving the door open is nice, but it's not enough. Some people don't even know the door exists, or they've been told all their life that they don't belong on the other side of it. So don't just prop it open—walk back, grab somebody by the hand, and guide them through. Show them the ropes. Introduce them to the right people. Give them the confidence to stand tall in the room. Because legacy isn't about being the only one who made it—it's about making sure you're not the last.

If you don't remember anything else from this book, remember this: legacy isn't about what you leave *to* people—it's about what you leave *in* them. Titles fade, plaques collect dust, but the seeds you plant in people last forever. Real leadership isn't about hogging the mic—it's about knowing when to pass it, and doing it with confidence, care, and intention. Open doors, keep them open, and then walk people through so they know they belong on the other side. Because your power doesn't shrink when you share it—it multiplies. Real leaders don't just take up space… they *make* space. Period.

REFLECTIONS

"LEADERSHIP IS NOT PEOPLE-
PLEASING. IT'S DECISION-MAKING. IF
CLARITY MAKES YOU THE VILLAIN,
WEAR THE CAPE."

CLOSING MESSAGE

If you've made it to this point, I want you to really hear me: nothing changes just because you read a book. Things change when you decide you're done leading on autopilot and start doing the work on yourself for real. You don't need to become a different person — you need to become a more honest version of who you already are. Honest about your limits. Honest about your patterns. Honest about the places where you've been shrinking, overextending, or hiding behind "busy."

You don't have to be perfect to lead well. You just have to be real, consistent, and willing to grow — even when it's uncomfortable and nobody's clapping for you. Leadership will stretch you, confront you, and sometimes expose parts of you that you'd rather not deal with. Don't run from that. Sit with it. That tension you feel is where the next level of you is trying to break through.

As you leave these pages and step back into your life, my challenge to you is simple: protect your peace, honor your boundaries, and lead with a clear spine and a steady heart. Say no when you need to. Say yes when it aligns. Have the hard conversations you've been avoiding. Stop trying to save everyone at the cost of losing yourself. The people around you don't need a perfect leader — they need a healthy one.

Your title may change. Your roles may shift. Seasons will come and go. But the work you do on yourself will follow you into every room you ever lead in. That's your real influence. That's your real legacy.

So go forward with clarity, with courage, and with a willingness to grow — again and again. Keep your boundaries. Keep your humanity. Keep showing up as yourself.

I'll see you at your next level.

"PROFESSIONAL RESPECT IS BUILT
WHERE CLEAR STANDARDS ARE
COMMUNICATED AND CONSISTENTLY
UPHELD."

A VERY SPECIAL THANK YOU

Thank You!

Thank you for purchasing **Boundaries in Business: The Playbook for Mindful Leadership**. It means a lot that you chose to invest your time, energy, and attention into this work. My hope is that something in these pages challenged you, affirmed you, or gave you language for things you were already feeling. Most of all, I hope you walk away clearer, steadier, and more committed to honoring yourself while you lead others.

I'd love to stay connected with you beyond this book. Visit **www.deblairtate.com** to stay up to date with what's happening next, upcoming events, programs, and new resources I'm creating. While you're there, you can also join my community and continue the conversation around leadership, growth, and boundaries.

You can also follow me on social media:

- **Instagram:** @iamdeblair
- **LinkedIn:** DeBlair F. Tate

To **join the community directly from your phone**, do this now:

Using your cell phone, text the keyword **8Figured** to **770-685-6709** in the text message box and hit send. Then follow the prompts to add your information, and you'll receive the community contact afterward so you can save it in your phone.

Thank you again for being here, for doing the work, and for committing to becoming the kind of leader who leads with clarity, courage, and boundaries. I'm grateful you're part of this journey.

"LEADERSHIP REQUIRES THE DISCIPLINE TO SAY NO TO WHAT IS MISALIGNED, EVEN WHEN IT IS PROFITABLE."

ABOUT THE AUTHOR

DeBlair Tate wears many hats and wears them well. She's a Health & Wellness Coach, Life Coach, Author, Master Resilience Trainer, former Military Training Instructor, and the visionary behind the 8Figured Brand. But beyond the titles, she's a woman on a mission—to help people build confidence, own their worth, and prioritize their health without apology or guilt.

Her message is simple but powerful: live with intention. Whether it's your choices, your habits, or your purpose, DeBlair believes that every step should line up with your values. Integrity, loyalty, relationships, and good health aren't just words for her—they're the core of how she leads, how she serves, and how she pushes others to level up.

In addition to coaching and training, CMSgt DeBlair Tate serves as Headquarters AFRC MAJCOM Functional, Equal Opportunity, United States Air Force. She's a 2X published author with *Resilient As F*ck: How To Fight For What You Deserve* and *Level Up: 325 Days to Empowered Living*. She's also a dynamic speaker who knows how to light up a stage, whether at the Essence Festival in New Orleans or in rooms where leaders are built and inspired.

Her influence doesn't stop there. DeBlair has collaborated

with ShellGasUS on a nationwide campaign, landed features on CNN, Fox Business Magazine, Atlanta Voice, and countless podcasts, livestreams, and radio shows. Her 8Figured Brand even caught the spotlight on *Good Morning America*. She's been honored by Fulton County's commissioner during Women's History Month with her own dedicated day, and her story has been highlighted by *Now This* for the impact she's making on the world.

Beyond the accolades, DeBlair stays connected to her community as a proud member of Delta Sigma Theta Sorority, Inc. and as an owner of an all-female motorcycle club. Whether she's riding with her sisters, coaching clients, or commanding respect in the military, one thing is constant: DeBlair Tate shows up with purpose, passion, and power.